THE
SLEEP BOOK

THE SLEEP BOOK

by
Shirley Motter Linde
and
Louis M. Savary

A Collins Associates Book

HARPER & ROW, PUBLISHERS

NEW YORK, EVANSTON, SAN FRANCISCO, LONDON

FIRST EDITION

ISBN 0–06–065249–7

LIBRARY OF CONGRESS CATALOG CARD NUMBER: 73 7066

ACKNOWLEDGMENTS

Many of the works from which selections herein are taken are protected by copyright, and may not be reproduced in any form without the consent of the authors, their publishers, or their agents. Every effort has been made to trace the ownership of all selections in this book and to obtain the necessary authorization for their use. If any errors or omissions have occurred in this regard, corrections will be made in all future editions of this book. Since the copyright page cannot legibly accommodate all the acknowledgments and copyright notices, this page and the pages following constitute an extension of the copyright page.

The authors wish to express sincere appreciation to the following organizations and individuals for their help in the preparation and review of material contained in this book.

Abbott Laboratories
    Abbott Park, North Chicago, Illinois: Thomas A. Craig, Manager, Professional Relations Dept.

American Psychiatric Association
    Washington, D.C.

Arthur M. Arkin, M.D.
    Department of Psychology, City College of the City University of New York, New York, N.Y.

Dr. Arthur R. Arkin

Eugene Aserinsky, Ph.D.
    Professor of Physiology, Jefferson Medical College of Thomas Jefferson University.

Dr. Bruno Bettelheim
    University of Chicago, Ill.

Alton Blakeslee
    New York, N.Y.

D. Robert Brebbia, Ph.D.
    Director, Neuro-Metabolic Laboratory Research Center, Rockland State Hospital, Orangeburg, N.Y

Rachel Carr
    New York, N.Y.

Patricia Carrington, Ph.D.
    Department of Psychiatry, New York Medical College.

William C. Dement, M.D., Ph.D.
    Director, Sleep Laboratories, Department of Psychiatry, Stanford University School of Medicine, Stanford, Calif.

Downstate Medical Center of The State University of New York
    Brooklyn, N.Y.

Duke University Medical Center
    Durham, N. C.

Dr. Jan Ehrenwald

Harmon S. Ephron, M.D.
    Department of Psychiatry, New York Medical College.

Dr. Ann Faraday
    London University.

Roland Fischer
    Professor of Experimental Psychiatry, Associate Professor of Pharmacology, Ohio State University College of Medicine, Columbus, Ohio.

Charles Fisher, M.D.
    Director, Sleep Laboratory, Mt. Sinai School of Medicine, New York, N. Y. Mt. Sinai Hospital, Institute of Psychiatry, Department of Psychiatry, New York, N. Y.

David Foulkes
    Psychology of Sleep.

Sigmund Freud

Robert Gaines
    New York, N. Y.

Russell Gardner, M.D.
    Assistant Professor of Psychiatry, Albert Einstein College of Medicine, at Montefiore Hospital and Medical Center.

Dr. Harry Gershman
    Dean, Training and Supervising Analyst of The American Institute for Psychoanalysis of the Karen Horney Psychoanalytic Institute and Center.

Rheta B. Glueck
    The Mount Sinai Medical Center, New York, N. Y.

Dr. Alan Grey
    Fordham University, New York, N. Y.

Wyman Guin
    New York, N. Y.

Calvin Hall

Ernest Hartmann, M.D.
    Associate Professor of Psychiatry, Tufts University School of Medicine; Director, Sleep and Dream Laboratory, Boston State Hospital.

Mrs. Jean C. Jones
    Librarian, American Psychiatric Museum Association, Washington, D.C.

Carl Jung

Edwin Kahn, Ph.D., Charles Fisher, M.D.

Adele Edwards, B.A. and David M. Davis, B.S.
   Department of Psychiatry, Mount Sinai School of
   Medicine of The City University of New York, N. Y

Anthony Kales, M.D.
   Director, UCLA Sleep Research and Treatment
   Facility, Los Angeles, Calif.

Donald Kalsched
   Fordham University, New York, N. Y.

Dr. Joe Kamiya
   Langley Porter Institute, San Francisco, Calif.

Ismet Karacan, M.D., D.Sc.
   Director, Sleep Research Laboratories, University of
   Florida Medical School, Gainesville, Fla.

Nathaniel Kleitman, M.D.
   Santa Monica, Calif.

Stanley Krippner, Ph.D.
   Director, Dream Laboratory, Maimonides Medical
   Center, Brooklyn, New York, N. Y.

Albert A. Kurland, M.D.
   Director, Maryland Psychiatric Research Center,
   Baltimore, Md.

Dr. Stuart Lewis,
   Edinburgh, Scotland.

Morton Lipshutz
   Assistant to Director, Medical Communications,
   Wyeth Laboratories, Division of American Home
   Products Corporation, Philadelphia, Pa.

Gay Gaer Luce

Dr. Alvin R. Mahrer
   Director, Clinical Psychology Program, Miami
   University, Fla.

Gilbert F. Martin
   American Medical Association, Chicago, Ill.

The Mount Sinai Hospital
   Sleep Laboratory
   New York, N. Y.

R. D. Nelson
   The Central Premonitions Registry.

I. H. Paul, Ph.D. and Charles Fisher, M.D., Ph.D.
   Department of Psychiatry, Mount Sinai Hospital,
   New York, N. Y.

Pfizer Inc.
   Groton, Conn.

A. H. Robins Company
   Richmond, Va.

Roscoe E. Puckett, Jr.

Allan Rechtschaffen, Ph. D.
   Professor, Departments of Psychiatry and Psychology
   Sleep Laboratory, University of Chicago, Ill.

Dr. Louisa Rhine
   Institute of Parapsychology, Durham, N. C.

Mary Rolfe
   Association for the Advancement of Psychoanalysis
   of the Karen Horney Psychoanalytic Institute and
   Center, New York, N. Y.

Bendrich Roth, M.D.
   Department of Neurology, Charles University
   Medical Faculty, Prague, Czechoslovakia.

Julius Segal, Ph.D.
   National Institute of Mental Health.

Howard Shevrin, Ph.D.
   Senior Psychologist, The Menninger Foundation,
   Topeka, Kan.

Jay Shurley, M.D.
   Behavioral Sciences Laboratory, Veterans Administration Hospital, Oklahoma City, Okla.

Dr. Frederick Snyder
   Chief of the NIMH Section on Psychophysiology of
   Sleep.

Loretta Tango
   Public Relations, Ciba-Geigy Corporation, Summit,
   N.J.

Dr. Montague Ullman
   Maimonides Hospital, Brooklyn, New York, N. Y.

U.S. Department of Health, Education, and Welfare
   Public Health Service, National Institute of Health,
   Bethesda, Md.; National Institute of Mental Health,

R. L. Van de Castle, Ph.D.
   Director, Sleep and Dream Laboratory, University of
   Virginia Medical School, Charlottesville, Va.

Wallace Pharmaceuticals
   Division of Carter-Wallace, Inc., Cranbury, N. J.:

Wilse B. Webb, Ph.D. and Harman W. Agnew, Jr., M.A.
   University of Florida, Gainesville, Fla.

Herbert Weiner, M.D.
   Professor and Chairman, Department of Psychiatry,
   Albert Einstein College of Medicine; Division of
   Psychiatry, Montefiore Hospital and Medical Center,
   Bronx, N. Y.

Albert Weissman, Ph.D.
   Assistant Director of Pharmacology, Pfizer Inc.,
   Groton, Conn.

Elliot D. Weitzman, M.D.
   Chief, Department of Neurology, Montefiore
   Hospital, Bronx, N. Y.

Robert L. Williams, M.D.
   Department of Psychiatry, College of Medicine of
   The University of Florida, Gainesville, Fla.; Veterans
   Administration Hospital, Gainesville, Fla.

Herman A. Witkin
   Educational Testing Service, Princeton, N. J.

William W. K. Zung
   Department of Psychiatry, Veterans Administration
   Hospital; Department of Psychiatry, Duke University
   Medical Center, Durham, N. C.

Contents

USING AND MISUSING SLEEP TIME

REMEDIES FOR INSOMNIACS

DEALING WITH OTHER SLEEP PROBLEMS

PART II: PRACTICE

EXPLORING RHYTHMS

GETTING READY

DROPPING OFF

DREAMWORLDS

Theory

JOURNEY INTO SLEEP

EXPLORING SLEEP

Everyone sleeps. Sleep — letting the self enter into the dark side of consciousness — binds together all people — indeed, all creatures of the world.

At birth, people emerge from the depths of non-awareness; they end in the darkness of death, the eternal sleep. And during every day of life in between there occurs the rhythm of night and day, of sleep and waking, the circadian rhythm to which everyone is subject.

About one third of the human lifetime is spent in the rhythmic coming and going of sleep; and yet how little we know of it!

Sleep is interwoven with every facet of daily life. It is involved in personal growth and development; it affects health and well-being, moods and behavior, energy and emotions, sanity and psychosis. It helps shape a person's very life style. It is necessary to attention and learning, to work and happiness.

Sleep serves purposes far more extensive than mere mind and body restoration. There is, in fact, hardly an aspect of waking life which is not affected by it, and people have barely begun to realize its potential for ensuring healthier, more fulfilled waking hours.

In Bed

In bed we laugh; in bed we cry; in bed are born; in bed we die; the near approach the bed doth show, of human bliss to human woe.

Isaac de Benserade

The Pleasures of Sleep

Blessings on him that first invented sleep! It covers a man, thoughts and all, like a cloak; it is meat for the hungry, drink for the thirsty, heat for the cold, and cold for the hot. It is the current coin that purchases cheaply all the pleasures of the world, and the balance that sets even king and shepherd, fool and sage.

Miguel de Cervantes Saavedra

And yet in sleep hides a mystery world, the dark unknown regions of consciousness, still mostly uncharted and unexplored.

Poets and philosophers frequently speak about this most secret part of life. Fairy tales explore its mystery: *Jack and the Beanstalk, Little Bo Peep, Rip Van Winkle, Alice in Wonderland, Sleeping Beauty*. The mention of sleep in literature calls to

Man Lives in Sleep

Man does not see the real world. The real world is hidden from him by the wall of imagination. He lives in sleep.

George Gurdjieff

mind such characters as Lady Macbeth, Brünhilde, Don Quixote, Old Testament heroes cut down in their tents.

And dreams! Dickens has David Copperfield describe more than twenty dreams in his novel. Chaucer was fascinated with dreams and repeatedly wove them into his tales. Freud spent a lifetime studying them.

Artists, too, have been intrigued by sleep. Renaissance painters and sculptors showed dreamers beset by visions and visitations from enemies attacking during sleep. Picasso's Blue Period favored sleepers and sleeping, painting after painting exploring the theme of one person watching another sleep.

Why do people sleep? What controls this universal cycle that is as sure as the coming of seasons, predictable as the ebb and flow of tides, familiar as night following day? What do we really know about what happens on the other side of our consciousness, in sleep?

Because of the mystery surrounding sleep and dreams, many beliefs have arisen that simply are not true. For example, that the brain rests during sleep, or that there is only one undifferentiated kind of sleep. On the other hand, some very wild stranger-than-fiction things *are* true. For example, that scientists can tell exactly when a person is dreaming, and that 30 million people in America suffer from insomnia.

People enjoy hearing long-held myths about sleep and dreams just as much as they delight in certain strange facts that defy explanation and unexplained observations that mystify scientists. So these pages include ancient myths and folklore as well as some facts very recently discovered in research laboratories throughout the world.

The Subconscious Mind

Even during sleep, the subconscious mind continues active . . . The subconscious mind is more active in that stage where the conscious mind is subjugated to physical laws, such as in sleep.

Edgar Cayce

Our Other Self

No one who does not know himself can know others. And in each of us there is another whom we do not know. He speaks to us in dreams and tells us how differently he sees us from the way we see ourselves. When, therefore, we find ourselves in a difficult situation to which there is no solution, he can sometimes kindle a light that radically alters our attitude—the very attitude that led us into the difficult situation.

C. G. Jung

15

RESEARCHERS OF INNER SPACE

A sleep laboratory looks not too unlike any other laboratory. But as much research is done there in the silence of the night as in busy daytime.

The lab contains a bed for sleeping, and nearly every night a volunteer subject sleeps there while scientists tune in on his brain. They are exploring the mind's inner space, asking questions such as: What makes the brain work? What moves it into the unconsciousness of sleep? What happens to it during sleep? And what happens to waking consciousness during the sleeping hours?

The inner space of the brain holds more components, more complexities and more mysteries than the entire universe of outer space with its billions of stars.

Part of the universe sleep researchers explore are the brain cells — millions of living units pulsing with energy and transmitting signals. Tiny electrical impulses speed from cell to cell, to brain centers and back again, carrying their messages. Sleep scientists probe brain activity by recording these electrical signals. Their tool is the electroencephalograph — EEG for short.

Brain recordings are fairly simple to obtain. The subject sits in a chair, or — for sleep studies — stretches out comfortably on a laboratory bed, while a nurse pastes tiny metal strips on a dozen places around the top and back of the head. These metal strips, called electrodes, pick up electrical discharges coming from brain cells. From each electrode a wire runs to the electroencephalograph machine.

The EEG machine is about the size of a desk, but it displays enough dials and controls to give the feeling of a scene in a science fiction film. It's similar to an electrocardiograph which records heartbeats, but the EEG is ten times as complicated and a hundred times as sensitive.

Once the EEG electrodes are connected, the doctor flips a switch, and eight pens start scratching back and forth on a moving roll of paper, making long scribbly lines of irregular waves and peaks and wiggles. Recordings are made while the subject's eyes are open, then while closed, awake and asleep. At the end of the recording session, doctors scrutinize the recorded roll. They pull it through their fingers and read each detail much as the financier handles ticker tape from the stock exchange.

What they see on the brain wave chart tells them much of the brain's inner workings and the ways in which it acts differently during the various stages of sleep. The charts even help doctors discern differences in certain types of brain damage and mental illness.

Brain wave charts represent the brain's computing apparatus at work — an apparatus so complex that a comparable man-made computer would require a five-story building many blocks long to house it. The brain's computer contains over 15 billion nerve cells. With long arm-like fibres, cells link together in an overlapping interweaving jungle of switchboard connections. Messages of pain, smell, hot or cold, run, relax, scream, or remember flash over the connections at 200 miles per hour.

Electrical discharges between brain cells seem to beat in rhythm like far-off native drums, charging and discharging, pulsing, constantly repeating, even when people are asleep.

In a Sleep Laboratory

A visit to a sleep laboratory is invaluable in understanding the fascinating discoveries that keep coming from this new science. Here — where one can see the sleepers, the wires taped about their heads, and actually watch the electronic machines tracing out the individual rhythms of brain waves and various muscular movements in coordinated patterns — one begins to comprehend the possibilities of dream research. Even the inexperienced eye can quickly detect the distinctive difference between the waking tracing and the various stages of sleep.

Morton T. Kelsey

They were first discovered in 1929 by Hans Berger, an eccentric German psychiatrist who did his work in secret. To produce changes in brain waves, he made his subjects sleepy with beer and woke them up by exploding firecrackers. Among his colleagues, Dr. Berger and his brain waves were considered slightly ridiculous — until other doctors experimented and confirmed his findings.

Today, EEG machines are used throughout the world for diagnosis and research. A million miles of paper have been covered with brain wave patterns since 1929.

Because of their complexity, EEG machines are often tricky. They have been known to pick up short-wave broadcasts of taxicabs, police cars, ship-to-shore calls, radar signals and the Democratic National Convention. But they also provide a unique way of looking into unexplored areas: the brain awake, sleeping, dreaming, remembering. One research team even took a machine to India to study the brain waves of Yogis.

Other researchers use machines that can record from dozens of brain areas at one time, or insert wire electrodes directly into the brain to probe responses from deeper brain layers. There are electronic analyzers that break brain wave patterns into separate parts to simplify interpretation, and an instrument called a toposcope that shows the brain's electrical activity by employing a series of flashing lights on television-like screens.

Besides the EEG, sleep researchers frequently use two other measuring devices. One is the electro-oculogram (EOG), which measures the presence of rapid eye movements (REM). The other, called electromyogram (EMG), measures impulses and movements in bodily muscles indicating the amount of ongoing muscle activity.

Dreaming and Sign Language

Dr. Samuel Grindley Howe, Superintendent of the Perkins Institute and Massachusetts Asylum for the Blind, taught the deaf, dumb, and blind Laura Bridgman a hand and finger language. He states (in one of the annual reports of the Institute) that even in her dreams Laura talked to herself using the finger language with great rapidity.

J. B. Watson

Early and Later Dreams

Ordinarily, the first dream of the night tends to be related to current problems. Dreams later in sleep tend to refer to incidents in childhood and adolescence — in other words, are usually flashbacks of some kind. The dreams of early morning often return to current events.

A sleep fact

Sleep and I.Q.

Young children with higher I.Q.s sleep less on the average than children who are not as bright.

A sleep fact

Explaining Mental Disorders

It is quite likely . . . that a modification of our attitude towards dreams will at the same time affect our views upon the internal mechanism of mental disorders, and that we shall be working towards an explanation of the psychoses while we are endeavouring to throw some light on the mystery dreams.

Sigmund Freud

A special sleep analyzer, developed by the National Aeronautics and Space Administration, was used on astronauts aboard NASA's Skylab. The sleep analyzer records EEG signals, as well as eye movement and other activities of the body. Three prototype models are now in experimental use at the University of South Carolina Medical School, at the University of Texas, and at the Veterans Administration Hospital in Oklahoma City.

Already the apparatus has proved valuable in research involving treatment of insomnia, study of sleep in pilots after unusually stressful duty, sleep patterns in drug addicts, side effects of new drugs being developed, and sleep characteristics of burn- and brain injury victims. An analyzer sits atop a 17,000 foot mountain peak on the Alaska-Canada border, measuring sleep patterns of subjects living at high altitudes.

The REM Discovery

The discovery of the REM state gave rise to a great resurgence of interest in all aspects of the study of sleep, and any generalizations about sleep based upon earlier investigations should now be re-examined.

Dr. F. Snyder

During Alpha Activity

According to recent research a subject with eyes taped open, while in the alpha phase, is likely to be functionally blind. That is, he is quite unable to report the nature of various objects that an experimenter may wave before his open and slowly moving eyes.

A sleep fact

HUMAN RHYTHMS

Sleep is one of many natural rhythms that affect humans.

Nature moves in rhythms and cycles. There is rhythm in the way the sun comes up and the way the moon comes out. Seasons follow a predictable cycle, the buds in spring, the leaves dropping in fall. A "biological time clock" in every plant and animal controls when they wake, when they grow tired, when they carry on their activities.

People have daily and weekly cycles as well as longer ones, basically monthly, over which physical strength as well as emotions wax and wane. Some keep regular charts of their ups and downs as carefully as others watch horoscopes. One surgeon schedules operations according to the strongest periods in his patients' individual cycles.

Most human rhythms are circadian, or daily cycles, revolving like the earth around the sun in a 24-hour pattern. Of these rhythms sleep is the most regular, normally recurring every day of people's lives. Scientists have learned some fascinating things about the sleep rhythm.

For example, they experimented with a person's sense of timing in a situation where there was no daylight or night to follow, no sunrise or sunset, no watches or clocks.

One young French geologist, Michel Siffre, decided to isolate himself in a cave where the daily rhythm of light and darkness was not observable. In the Alps, at over 7,500 feet, he found an icy, wet cave that he could reach only by lowering himself into a long narrow hole that descended vertically for 90 feet, snaked around in an S-shaped tunnel, then dropped further to an underground depth of about 400 feet. The cave was in total darkness. The floor was solid ice, the air foggy, the temperature freezing.

Michel Siffre was lowered by rope and ladder into the long tunnel-like hole, and on the icy floor he

pitched a tent. For two months, completely alone, he remained there with no way of telling whether it was day or night, time to wake up or go to sleep, time for breakfast or dinner, whether it was still today or already tomorrow.

His only contact was by telephone with two friends at the surface. He called to tell them when he went to bed, when he woke up and when he ate a meal. He kept a diary of his activities and a chart of the time and day he thought it was, while his friends kept a corresponding chart of the *actual* time.

After the experiment was over, they compared the two charts and found that Siffre had guessed wrong on how many days he had spent in the cave, and had mis-estimated the amount of time he spent working. For example, during periods when he guessed he had worked 4 to 5 hours, he had actually worked 10 to 12 hours. But generally he judged his hours of sleep correctly. And, amazingly enough, his sleep time plus working and waking time averaged out at 24 hours — even though he didn't have a clock to guide him.

With no alteration of darkness and light, with no clock, with irregular meals, his body still kept a 24-hour day!

The well-known sleep researcher, Nathaniel Kleitman, carried out a similar cave experiment with a young assistant. The assistant was able to make adjustments. Dr. Kleitman, older, could not.

When people try to change built-in sleep rhythms, they often find it difficult to adjust. Day shift workers in a factory who switch to the night shift at first find they're eating breakfast when they used to eat dinner, and trying to work at peak efficiency when their bodies are yawning for bed. After a time, biological time clocks adjust to the new timing; but workers who keep switching back and forth from night shift to day shift can become extremely inefficient and nervous, and sometimes even have need of medical treatment.

To Comfort and Cheer Me

There have been times in my life when I fell asleep with tears in my eyes, but in my dreams the most delightful visions came to me to comfort and cheer me, and the next morning I would rise again feeling fresh and happy.

Goethe

People who jet across several time zones face a major change in sleep's daily rhythm. This is a common problem for stewardesses, pilots and overseas airline passengers. Those who take long east-west trips (it doesn't happen on a north-south trip) may find that when they arrive for an important appointment — when they would like to be sharp and alert — their body is rebelling and adjusting; they feel tired and worn-out.

Also, people crossing time zones often find that despite their fatigue they have trouble sleeping. Others report that their brains are foggy, they have trouble concentrating, they become irritable, their reactions are slow, and they experience stomach and intestinal problems. Doctors call this the time-zone fatigue syndrome.

Studies have been done on overseas-traveling businessmen, actors, chess players, athletes and even race horses. None of them operates at optimum level for the first few days after arrival. Neither do race horses. It takes three, sometimes four days to return to normal. Knowing the probable bad effects of crossing several time zones is important, for example, to a pilot landing a plane full of people, or to a diplomat who on arrival will be making important decisions in foreign policy. Pilots on long jet flights are now limited to flying a regulated number of hours at one time and only a certain number of hours a month.

Those who need good judgment cannot afford to be tired. People taking a trip that crosses many time zones are well advised not to make decisions during the first 24 hours after arrival. If a meeting is really important, get there several days early and sleep. One international traveling executive of a major airline says he's not bothered so much by jet fatigue while traveling, but is disturbed by extremely vivid dreams whenever he returns from such trips.

Scientists have found that even migrating birds never cross more than four time zones without allowing time for their natural sleep rhythms to readjust.

Monotony Causes Sleep

You will fall asleep faster in a monotonous situation than when exposed to complete silence and darkness. This was shown in Marseilles when 150 people were tested, some confined to a dark and silent room, some in the same room but with four minutes of a monotonous repetitive flash of light or noise. More than a third of the second group fell asleep in less than four minutes. In the other group, almost no one fell asleep.

A sleep fact

GOING INTO SLEEP

What actually happens when someone falls asleep? What does the brain do? Where does waking consciousness go? As the sleeper loses awareness of his surroundings and drifts off into feathery fuzziness and weightlessness, then further down into the night of deep sleep, what really is happening?

Scientists who monitor this hidden side of our daily life learned that sleep is not all black darkness, not a uniform time of emptiness. Actually, there are many different kinds of sleep, each functioning at a different depth of consciousness. Every sleeper every night passes through lighter and darker shades of sleep, rising and falling upon them as a quiet boat rides on irregular waves.

A sleeper in the bedroom — quiet, passive, removed — hardly betrays the busy brain activity going on within. But in the sleep labs EEG recordings clearly document it.

In the control room, a researcher keeping his night-long vigil over a sleeper in the laboratory, charts the brain activity as the subject passes through various stages of sleep. Sometimes a sleeper may shift slowly from one level of sleep to another; at other times the change is quicker, taking only minutes or seconds.

Dr. Wilse B. Webb, research psychologist at the University of Florida, describes the sleep state as a house of several rooms among which the sleeper wanders back and forth irregularly and randomly during the night.

"Picture four rooms," he suggests, "one behind the other (Stages 1, 2, 3, and 4). Off the room labeled '2' is a porch, labeled 'REM'." (REM, the sleep state characterized by Rapid Eye Movement, is the period in which most remembered dreaming takes place.) During the sleeper's night occurs considerable scurrying back and forth among the rooms, Webb explains, with an average of 35 sleep-stage changes during a typical night of inner wandering.

The Knack of Falling Asleep

How do people go to sleep? I'm afraid I've lost the knack. I might try busting myself smartly over the temple with the nightlight. I might repeat to myself, slowly and soothingly, a list of quotations beautiful from minds profound; if I can remember any of the damn things.

Dorothy Parker

Just Before Falling Asleep

Almost everyone has experienced the sudden body jerk that occurs just as one falls asleep. Some people say they also see a flash of light, hear a bang or a musical note, or have a feeling of falling at the same time. Scientists have shown that this always occurs when the alpha rhythm has been absent for a few seconds and small slow waves have started up.

A sleep fact

Sleep and the Higher Self

Our higher self does not sleep; therefore it can and will take note of and act upon suggestions and directions given to it as we drop off to sleep.

Mary Ann Woodward

Plants at Nightfall

Plants usually give no evidence of night-time changes, but interiorly follow a cyclic period of dormancy. For example, sweet corn picked at night will have a starchy taste, because the sugar in the ears flows downward through the stalk and into the roots at nightfall. At sunrise, the sugar flows freshly into the corn, which therefore tastes sweetest when picked then.

A sleep fact

Deep Sleep

Deep sleep — Stages 3 and 4 — occurs primarily during the early part of the night.

Most of the middle and late parts of the night are spent in REM sleep and Stage 2.

The amount of Stage 4 sleep is greatest in childhood, and decreases with age.

A sleep fact

"Sleepers do not enter rooms of their sleep house with predictable frequency, even on the average; neither do they remain in one room for a predictable period of time," says Dr. Webb. "Further, different sleepers favor certain rooms over others, and stay longer there than others."

Usually, he states, there is a systematic tendency to follow a consecutive sequence from Stage 1 to Stage 4 and back again, step by step, from Stage 4 to Stage 1; but frequently sleepers wander repeatedly between adjacent stages — for example, from 2 to 3, 3 to 2, 2 to 3. Each stage may last only seconds or minutes, but at times each of the four stages may endure for hours.

Webb describes Stage REM as a side porch, independent of the room sequencing. Typically (about 85 per cent of the time) the REM porch is attached to Stage 2 — that is, the sleeper enters and leaves REM from the second stage. The REM condition, an indication that the sleeper is dreaming, occurs and recurs with no clearly discernible pattern other than that REM periods are more frequent later in sleep — after the first hour or so.

In a typical night's sleep, relaxation and drowsiness initiate the process. Body temperature starts to drop, eyes close, brain waves begin a regular pattern known as alpha rhythm. The subject experiences a state of relaxed wakefulness, or serenity. This state of resting with eyes-closed-but-sleep-not-yet-started is called Stage 0 by some sleep scientists. A moment of tension, or an attempt to solve a mental problem may disrupt it, and return the would-be sleeper to full wakefulness.

With further relaxation the alpha waves grow smaller, decreasing in amplitude, and the subject drifts between drowsiness and sleep, perhaps seeing images, experiencing dreamlike thoughts or fragments. This is called the hypnagogic state and the visualizations that occur during it are termed hypnagogic images.

Another pattern begins to emerge on the EEG graph paper — smaller, with lower voltages. Its tracings appear uneven, desynchronized, fast, irregular and swiftly changing. This is Stage 1 of sleep. It may involve a floating sensation, drifting with idle images. Body muscles relax, respiration grows more even, and heart rate slows down. A person can be easily awakened from Stage 1 by a slight noise or spoken word and the sleeper may even assert that he was not really asleep. This phase of consciousness acts as a port of entry to deeper sleep, a borderland to be crossed, and lasts only a few minutes.

Soon the background rhythm of the EEG grows slower, and the brain wave tracings grow larger, displaying quick bursts of rapid waves known as spindles, like momentary crescendos and decrescendos in a musical performance. The eyes may appear to be slowly rolling. The person in Stage 2 is soundly asleep, yet can be awakened with little difficulty. However, the Stage 2 sleeper will usually not be disturbed by turning on a light in the room.

Soon the person drifts deeper, into Stage 3. Here the EEG records spindle-bursts and irregular brain waves interspersed with large slow waves, occurring at about one a second. Now it will take a loud noise to awaken the sleeper. His muscles are almost totally relaxed, he breathes evenly, and his heart rate becomes even slower than before. Blood pressure is falling, and temperature continues to decline.

Eventually he slips into Stage 4, the deepest level of sleep. In this stage, the muscles are completely relaxed and the sleeper rarely moves. It is harder to awaken him, heart rate and temperature are still declining, respiration is slow and even, and if you do awaken him with a loud noise, he may come into focus slowly, and may report no experience of mental activity. The EEG shows a continuous pattern of slow, synchronized, high-amplitude waves. It reports brain response to outside stimuli such as sounds, but these do not seem to reach the conscious level.

If sleepwalking occurs, it happens during Stage 4. It is in this stage, too, that children may wet their beds.

Deep sleep is a necessity for everyone. A normal person spends considerable sleep time in Stage 4, especially if he has lost sleep. And if annoyances hinder sufficient Stage 4 sleep, the sleeper will make up for his losses on subsequent nights.

About an hour or so after falling asleep and passing through the four stages, the sleeper may begin to drift back up into lighter phases. Usually after about an hour and a half of sleep, the EEG begins to scratch with wild oscillations.

As these oscillations die away the brain wave record may show an irregular low-voltage, rapidly changing pattern similar to that of Stage 1, and the eyes may begin to move back and forth rapidly, as if they were watching an event. These rapid eye movements, or REMs, mark the beginning of a vivid dreaming phase. It will take a relatively loud extraneous noise, such as heavy traffic or horns honking, to awaken a sleeper — yet a very slight noise with personal significance, such as the whimpering of a child, may quickly alert him.

"Although it may be hard to awaken a person at this time," says a government report, *Current Research on Sleep and Dreams,* "in many ways his brain activity paradoxically resembles waking, and REM sleep is often called paradoxical sleep. It is believed by some investigators to be a unique state, totally different from the rest of sleep, and subserved by different brain mechanisms."

Patterns of sleep vary with individuals and with age. For example, an infant enjoys 50 per cent REM sleep; some researchers even place it at 85 per cent. Yet within a year a baby's REM rate drops to 25 per cent of his sleep, where it remains for most of his life.

With Great Sincerity

I have, all my life long, been lying till noon, yet I tell all young men, and tell them with great sincerity, that nobody who does not rise early will ever do any good.

Samuel Johnson

As people grow older, the amount of Stage 4 sleep decreases, sometimes dropping to one-sixth of its original level; in some people it disappears altogether. With age, sleepers experience an increase in the amount of light sleep (Stage 1) as well as more broken sleep — that is, awakening during the night or surfacing to Stage Zero.

In the elderly, sleep often reverts to the infant's broken pattern of naps, confirming Shakespeare's seven stages of man, where the last stages involve a return to the first.

Each night's sleep patterns also are variable. Attempting to predict duration and frequency of various sleep stages in any one night only results in frustration for the investigator. The sleeping brain seems to have its own inner logic and language, and no one yet has deciphered even its REM rate. While researchers have some information, it remains confusing. For example, during a typical night, Stage 2 sleep may occur as often as 15 times or even more, but REM seldom occurs more than four or five times, usually unpredictably. As a rule, Stages 0, 1 and 3 are relatively short and transient stages. REM sleep periods, although occurring less frequently, usually last longer. Scientists are not sure why this happens.

REM sleep occurs mostly late in the sleep night while Stage 4 happens mostly during early sleep hours. Even when subjects are consistently deprived of REM sleep by being awakened after the first few hours, they still maintain the same Stage 4 pattern, experiencing this level predominantly during the first third of the night.

Two additional pieces of information about REM have been discovered. First, REM episodes occur at fairly regular intervals during the last third of sleep time, occurring about every 90 minutes, according to Drs. W. C. Dement and Nathaniel Kleitman. Second, despite long-held opinions to the contrary, REM sleep *does* occur during daytime naps.

What Heaven Has Joined

Life has married the unconscious and involuntary to the reasonable and spontaneous—and so man should not separate what heaven has joined.

Dr. Troxler

SLEEP AND THE BRAIN

Since the brain controls the sleep process, it is important to understand, at least in broad outline, its design and activity.

The brain has been described as a great computer, contact point of the spirit, center of the intellect, core of the emotions. In physical reality, however, what lies within the hard bony skull, protected by a thin, tough membrane and the protective fluid surrounding it, resembles a head of cauliflower — gray and convoluted, and a little mushy to the touch.

The brain is made up of billions of nerve cells, packed tightly together. In those billions of cells are stored memories, experiences, emotions, facts, beliefs and philosophies, reasoning — all the factors that help shape the personality. Also among those brain cells are centers that control body functions such as breathing, heartbeat, vision, hearing, speech — as well as waking and sleeping.

Most thinking and voluntarily controlled actions correspond to neural activity in the cerebral cortex at the top of the brain. Most brain cells that control routine behavior and more automatic functions are hidden in clusters located in deeper recesses within the lobes of the brain. Brain-research scientists worked for years hoping to find a cell cluster acting as control center for sleep.

With every tool they could devise, doing experiment after experiment with animals, researchers tried to locate within the brain a map of the still uncharted sleep system. With electrical impulses they stimulated various parts of the brain to see where such a sleep center might be. But, strangely, stimulation of *many different* brain regions seemed to produce sleep in animal subjects.

About 20 years ago, two doctors discovered that electrical stimulation of reticular cells deep inside the lower brain led to *arousal* of the animal and would

Brain Potentials

The brain is a continuously active electrical medium. It is possible to make recordings of its electrical activity without establishing physical contact with the brain surface itself. Tiny metal-disk electrodes are affixed to the scalp, usually with a collodion-impregnated gauze pad. These electrodes are sensitive to brain potentials, that is, moment-to-moment shifts in energy level between adjacent cells or regions of the cerebral cortex, the convoluted covering of the largest lobe of the human brain. The recording input of these electrodes is fed into an electroencephalograph.

A sleep fact

Sleep and Brainwashing

Brainwashing seems to rely heavily upon sleep deprivation as a technique for breaking down established patterns of thought and behavior.

A sleep fact

awaken it from sleep. They had discovered the arousal center of the brain.

Remember that in those days researchers considered sleep to be a *lack of consciousness*, the emptiness that happened when people weren't stimulated to stay awake. Scientists then believed that when the arousal center was stimulated, a person was awake and conscious, but when that center was not stimulated, the person fell asleep. According to their theory, sleep was defined simply as the lack of being awake.

But all theories are tentative, and this one has now been discounted. Today sleep is described not as a lack of activity, but as a different kind of activity, involving a different set of nerve cells, which actively *inhibits* the waking state and *causes* sleep. This current sleep theory corresponds to the usual working pattern of the nervous system: one set of nerves stimulating an activity, another set inhibiting that activity and stimulating another opposing one.

Scientists continued trying to map out the sleep system in the brain. They tested various microscopic brain areas with tiny amounts of chemicals as stimulants, and found that certain chemicals stimulated sleep and others blocked it.

Dr. Raoul Hernandez-Peon and his colleagues in Mexico City made one giant step when they found that sleep was regulated by a cluster of brain cells located along an extended region between the frontal area and the brain stem close to the spinal cord. By working painstakingly with chemicals and mapping electrode stimulations fractions of a millimeter apart over different areas and layers of the brain, they finally mapped out what seemed like the sleep network. It reached far forward to the frontal and temporal brain lobes, with the major sleep-regulating centers in the thalamus and the cerebellum, and some of the sleep nerves extending clear down into the brain stem near the spinal cord.

Further study of the sleep network showed that different clusters of brain cells were involved in different types of sleep. Touching certain areas of the network with a certain chemical, for example, determined how fast an animal would fall asleep. In one experiment, while a cat was eating its food, a researcher stimulated a certain sensitive spot in the sleep network. The cat fell asleep so fast that its face fell into the food!

Other brain areas seem to control how long the sleep lasts. Stimulate one area and an animal will sleep thirty minutes; stimulate another and he will sleep ten times as long.

Consequently, we now know that there is not one single sleep center, but an entire sleep roadway in the brain with connections to other neural layers involved in perception and thought. The spread and complexity of the sleep network may explain the many kinds of sleep people have, as well as how many outside conditions affect sleep. Sleep nerves seem to influence not only how fast we go to sleep, and how long we sleep, but how and why we decide it's time to go to sleep and how we feel about sleep. Hopefully, in time the intricate connections of the sleep network to

Four Sleep Stages

Stage 1 is the lightest sleep; Stage 4, the deepest. Awake and resting periods with eyes closed are often called Stage 0.

In young adults, 20 to 25 per cent of sleep is made up of REM, 50 per cent of Stage 2, 5 to 10 per cent of Stage 1, and 10 to 20 per cent of a combination of Stages 3 and 4.

A sleep fact

35

other systems will help explain how intense excitement or emotion or worry can keep us awake; why we become sleepy from such experiences as boredom, monotonous sounds, stroking, physical exhaustion, or sexual activity. Part of the sleep pathway also passes through the same bundle of fibres that lead to the recently discovered and much talked about pleasure center of the brain; this connection might explain why people often experience sleep as sensually pleasurable and satisfying.

One researcher, Dr. Eugene Aserinsky of Jefferson Medical College in Philadelphia, believes that there is also a "wakefulness chemical" in the body's sleeping apparatus — a substance that builds up during sleep, waking the person when it reaches a certain level, and then gradually disappears during waking hours until he again feels the need for sleep. If such a chemical can be isolated, states Aserinsky, people might be able to shorten or lengthen sleep time at will.

Some evidence for chemical control has come from research done by Dr. Werner P. Koella at the Worcester Foundation for Experimental Biology. Koella has been working with serotonin, a body chemical that plays a major part in many aspects of brain physiology. Serotonin is produced in particularly high concentrations in the hypothalamus, which contains one of the major centers controlling the level of consciousness. Coincidence? Or is serotonin possibly the transmitter chemical that regulates sleep?

In preliminary experiments, Koella found that serotonin injected into the cat's brain immediately

The Brain During Sleep

The brain can hear things when a person is asleep. It not only hears things, it can distinguish between different noises and different words.

Dr. I. Oswald and his sleep research colleagues studied sleeping people and found that if various names were spoken to them, they were able to distinguish their own name and react to it no matter how deeply asleep they were.

A sleep fact

36

caused the eye pupils to narrow, and within five to ten minutes the electroencephalograms displayed "slow" waves characteristic of deep sleep.

Later he experimentally deprived cats of serotonin by giving them PCPA, a drug that blocks the formation of serotonin. Normally, cats sleep about 15 hours a day; but Koella's cats, after receiving PCPA, spent only about 30 minutes of each day sleeping. Occasionally the cats would curl up as if to go to sleep, but would soon get up again and wander about restlessly and irritably. PCPA effects wore off after about eight or ten days and, as serotonin in their brains returned to normal levels, the cats resumed normal sleeping patterns.

Could a low serotonin level be one cause of insomnia? Dr. Koella thinks so, and he is now working on ways to raise the brain's serotonin level and produce "a truly physiological sleeping pill."

The most recent research has been done by Drs. Marcel Monnier and L. Hosli of the University of Basel, Switzerland, who have just announced possible discovery of a sleep hormone. They based their experiments on the idea that sleep could be transmitted from a sleeping animal to an alert one by transfer of some body chemical. They used a dialysate of brain blood from a sleeping rabbit, injected it into an alert rabbit, and it quickly fell asleep! The scientists are still a long way from knowing which blood compounds are the active ones, but they are perhaps at a first step in discovering a general sleep drug within the cerebral blood of a sleeping creature.

Brain Waves

Brain waves of 8-12 cycles per second (CPS) are called alpha activity; those of 12–14 CPS are called sleep spindles; those of 1-3 CPS are called delta activity. Theta activity is 4-7 CPS. Beta activity is beyond 14 CPS. In a resting period, most people have alpha activity.

A sleep fact

37

SLEEP AND THE BODY

What does it mean to say someone is asleep? What's happening in sleep?

People tend to think of sleep as a time of quiet, a time of complete inactivity. But during sleep a lot of activity is going on, both in the brain and in the body. Sleeping doesn't turn off major body systems; in fact some of them are more turned on during sleep than during wakefulness. This idea is so new that some medical textbooks only two or three years old are out of date because they haven't incorporated this new concept.

It is true that during the first one-and-a-half hours of sleep there is a decrease in heart and respiratory rate and a small drop in blood pressure. In fact, during sleep, respiration and pressure fall to their lowest levels of the day.

On the other hand, during REM sleep most activities of the brain and body actually *increase*! Cerebral blood flow accelerates, and some studies show that brain temperature actually rises. In REM, heart rate, blood pressure and respiration can sometimes fluctuate wildly. In fact, storms of activity and turbulence may occur during peak REM times, possibly accounting for heart attacks and other illnesses that happen during sleep.

Even hormone secretion is active during sleep, including a strong release of adrenal cortical hormone, of cortisol, and of growth hormone.

Lifespan and Sleepspan

Sleeping time of a species of animal seems to be related to its lifespan. Both bats and shrews, for example, are small, very active and have very high metabolic rates. The bat sleeps up to 20 hours a day, the shrew is busy, busy, busy, and seldom sleeps. The shrew lives about two years, The bat 18. Scientists think the difference is due to the bat's ability to sleep.

A sleep fact

An Orderly Cycle

Sleep is an orderly cycle involving bodily changes and altered states of consciousness, a unity of psychological and physiological transformations that is not separable from waking health and behavior.

Gay Gaer Luce

Kidneys produce less urine at night and pulse is slower, but our bodies continue to grow during sleep, replacing worn-out cells and storing energy. According to some researchers, skin does its growing mostly at night.

And man remains a sexual animal during sleep, usually experiencing erections at regular intervals during the night. Scientists report that during sleep erections occur on the average every 85 minutes and last for about 25 minutes. The arousal seems to occur in all males: infants, men in their 70s and 80s, and even some of those who complain of being impotent during waking hours.

Strangely enough, almost never does a volunteer subject have a nocturnal emission in the laboratory. Most researchers say it only happens about once a year out of hundreds of subjects brought in for testing. They feel that the laboratory setting has an inhibitory effect.

Occasionally an erection is lost suddenly during a dream, which typically has been found to be associated with an experience of anxiety or personal injury occurring in the dream. The penile erections, by the way, occur no matter what the dream content and do not necessarily have any relationship to sexual activity occurring in the dream.

At present, very little data exists on sexuality in women during sleep, but they also seem to experience periods of excitation during sleep. There is only preliminary research on women to determine whether they have any sexual reaction during REM parallel to the male's erections. It appears, although more work needs to be done, that an increase in nipple size and in blood supply to the vaginal area occur at intervals during the night, but do not seem to be connected with REM sleep.

While much physiological activity happens during sleep, what is of central interest to most people is the sleep activity called dreaming.

Ulcer Patients

Ulcer patients often wake up in the middle of the night with stomach pain. Reason: stomach acids increase their flow tremendously during REM dreams, often waking the person up with the pain produced. In addition, the ulcer patient secretes as much as 20 times more gastric acid during sleep than normal subjects. Drinking milk will usually neutralize the acid enough to eliminate the pain.

A sleep fact

THE LANGUAGE OF
DREAMS

REM AND DREAMS

In the nineteenth century a group of physicians reported their observations on two subjects who had a portion of skull removed, exposing the brain. They noted that the brain bulged out while the subject was dreaming, but returned to normal size when the dreaming ceased. In a similar situation, another scientist reported that brain convolutions began to swell during sleep whenever the sleeper's name was called.

In 1953 there occurred a breakthrough in the scientific study of dreams. At the University of Chicago, Dr. Nathaniel Kleitman, a world-famous sleep scientist, was conducting a sleep experiment on babies. One of his students, Eugene Aserinsky, noticed that at certain times during sleep the babies' eyes moved back and forth rapidly under closed eyelids. He and Kleitman then tested adult volunteers and observed the same eye movement. They speculated that rapid eye movements (REM) might be related to dreaming. In experiments they waited for these movements to appear in subjects during sleep — then woke the sleepers up. Results: Eighty per cent of the people awakened from REM sleep reported that they had been in the midst of vivid dreams when awakened. On the other hand, only 9 per cent of those awakened without REM reported dreaming.

Baby Sleep

In the newborn, 50 per cent of total sleep is spent in REM sleep.

A sleep fact

A little while later another student, William Dement, joined Kleitman at the Chicago laboratory. He discovered that the REM periods were accompanied by a brain wave pattern different from the brain waves of other periods of sleep.

Since the early days of Aserinsky and Dement, dozens of other sleep and dream labs have sprung up throughout the world, and dream research has increased to the point that scientists complain that they can no longer keep up with the hundreds of dream research reports that come out each year.

The excitement of that early period 20 years ago is mirrored in sleep researcher Dr. Allan Rechtschaffen's words:

"When I first arrived at the University of Chicago some 14 years ago, I chanced to be introduced to Edward Wolpert, then a medical student at the University. Wolpert had learned the REM research techniques from William Dement who had just completed his graduate and medical studies at Chicago. Wolpert told me a bit about this field of research — which I had not heard about until then — and invited me to observe an experiment of his own which he was conducting in Dr. Kleitman's laboratory. My first evening of observing Wolpert's experiment decided my choice of work from that time to the present. I remember Wolpert poised over an old four-channel Grass Model III EEG. (This historic machine was used by Aserinsky, Kleitman, Dement, Wolpert, Kamiya, Foulkes, and myself — in short, the whole first generation of Chicago REM researchers. The same machine is still in use in Chicago.) Wolpert showed me the rapid eye movements as they were traced on the moving paper and told me that when he awoke the subject we would hear a vivid dream report; that is exactly what happened. About a half hour later, Wolpert pointed out the spindles and lack of eye movements of Stage 2. He said that this time the subject would have nothing to report upon awakening, and that is just what happened. At that point, I said to myself something like, 'My God, here is the mind turning on and off during sleep, and we actually have a physiological indicator of when it is happening. What better opportunity is there to study how the mind and body are related?' "

REM Sleep Quota

The amount of REM sleep varies widely across species, but usually constitutes about 15 to 25 per cent of total sleep time. This has been demonstrated in hedgehogs, moles, shrews, several kinds of monkeys, pigs, ground squirrels, hamsters, rats and man. The greatest amount of REM sleep is found in the opposum (30 per cent). Mice and rabbits have about 10 per cent REM sleep, birds 5 to 10 per cent, and sheep only about 3 per cent.

A sleep fact

Evolutionary Sleep

REM sleep as we know it probably arose on the evolutionary scale about 130 million years ago.

A sleep fact

TWO KINDS OF DREAMING

Dreams were thought to be almost exclusive to the REM state until ten years ago. At that time, Dr. David Foulkes threw doubt on the theory by finding that anywhere from 23 to 74 per cent of non-REM sleep also produced some mental activity. Apparently when earlier researchers asked their subjects to report dreams, the awakened sleepers reported only vivid, exciting dreams. The dreams they had during non-REM they described as "just thinking". "Vivid and exciting" versus "just thinking" turned out to be the basic difference between REM dreaming and non-REM dreaming.

On the average, a person has three REM dreams per night. REM dreams are usually longer, more vivid, more visual, more dramatic, more detailed, more emotional, more active. Non-REM dreams tend to be the opposite: they appear shorter, less vivid and visual, less dramatic, less detailed, less emotional and active, but on the other hand are more believable, more concerned with current problems, more conversational, and more related to verbal thought processes.

Since a REM dream often involves several episodes and much detail — like a movie filled with drama and activity — the dreamer may need hundreds of words to narrate it completely. On the other hand, a non-REM dream might be described in a few sentences.

Devilish Dreams

There are two particular types of dreams initiated by the devil, one of which pertains to the disclosure and manifestation of occult secrets. For the devil can know and indicate to men through dreams the natural effects which will necessarily arise at any moment from certain causes, whatever he himself is about to do, and what things, both present and past, are hidden from men. The second type of dream has the power of exciting confusion in the mind so that when the humours and vapors which are in the body have been agitated and thrown off balance, men are excessively aroused, either to sensual pleasure, or to hate and vindictiveness, or to other perverse states of mind.

Benedict Pererius

In REM periods the dreamer is drawn deeply into a complete world of fantasy; he is difficult to awake and often feels he has been called back from some faraway place.

However, sometimes non-REM dreaming gives the dreamer a feeling of "wandering in a no-man's land," feeling lost or floating. Often he holds conversations with ghostlike characters. One person awakened from a non-REM period said, "I was walking, or rather floating, along a street, and there was someone floating toward me. I don't know who it was or where I was. I think I asked the person where I was. Gosh, it reminds me of T. S. Eliot's *Little Gidding* — you remember those lines — 'In the uncertain hour before the morning, Near the ending of interminable night . . . Between three districts whence the smoke arose I met one walking . . . As if blown towards me . . .' "

The non-REM dream seems to depict either a world that is strange, gray, shadowy, floating and mysterious — or one characterized by logical reasoning and thinking that makes the dreamer believe he is not asleep and dreaming, but really awake and thinking of things.

Sometimes dream thinking is not quite as clear as people experience it to be. Everyone remembers a dream where he discovered the key to the universe, the answer to life; and then it disappeared! This was probably a non-REM dream. One key-to-the-universe dreamer struggled to capture the words of such a revolutionary dream message and found that it read, "Readers who are opposed to a more exact coddling of the band than the situation warrants should fill in this form!"

Another dreamer believed he had finally found the perfect title for his new chemistry book. His dream title turned out to be *Twelve Bedsteads in Search of an Answer*. Occasionally short dreams also occur in the borderland period between wakefulness and sleep. Called hypnagogic dreams, they usually take the form of strange body sensations, conversations, and hallucinations. In this third form, dreams are similar to REM dreams in content, but are usually short-lived and are normally not accompanied by rapid eye movements.

Some people fascinated by hypnagogic imagery have trained themselves to prolong this period to explore their artistic creativity. Dr. Ann Faraday in her book *Dream Power* gives the following directions for those who want to learn to capture these dreamlets:

"Lie flat on your back in bed, but keep your arm in a vertical position, balanced on the elbow, so that it stays up with a minimum of effort. You can slip fairly easily and deeply into the hypnagogic state this way, but at a certain point, muscle tonus decreases, your arm falls down and wakes you up. Write down immediately whatever was going through your mind just prior to waking."

WHO DREAMS WHAT?

Women often place their dreams indoors; men's dreams are more likely set in the unfamiliar or outdoors. In dreams, women pay more attention to facial details, clothing, jewelry, household objects and flowers, while men more often mention automobiles, tools, weapons and money. There are more people in women's dreams, most often familiar ones. Men's dreams tend to involve unfamiliar people and they are often identified by occupation.

Men show more physical aggression in their dreams, while women usually report being victims of others' aggressions. Men mention more sex dreams, and dreams involving physical activity. Women are more likely to emphasize conversations and emotional reactions.

Among children, boys mention more implements, tools and things, while girls report longer dreams, more often with people in them. In their dreams children typically view themselves as victims of others, and their most frequent dream emotions are fear and apprehension, indicating tensions mirrored from waking hours.

Among small children the majority of dreams contain animals; but as they grow older the percentage of animal characters decreases. Adults dream of animals less than 8 per cent of the time. Dogs and horses are the most frequently dreamed of animals in both children and adults. Certain animals appear more frequently in children's dreams than in those of adults: These include lions, spiders, bears, gorillas, alligators, tigers and wolves.

Men Dream of the Outdoors

My dreams . . . are of architecture and of buildings — cities abroad, which I have never seen, and hardly have hoped to see. I have traversed, for the seeming length of a natural day, Rome, Amsterdam, Paris, Lisbon — their churches, palaces, market-places, shops, suburbs, ruins, with an inexpressible sense of delight — a maplike distinctness of trace — and a daylight vividness of vision that was all but being awake.

Charles Lamb

Pregnant women often dream of imagery involving seeds or fertility. One woman dreamed she was rowing across a river in an orange shell, found some magic seeds that quickly matured and became a plant. Often pregnant women also have terrifying or apprehensive dreams concerning their pregnancy and about their child being born deformed. Many of them are reluctant to discuss these dreams, fearing that others might interpret them as indicative of resentment at their pregnancy; instead such mothers-to-be silently suffer fear and guilt feelings.

Dreams during menstruation seem to contain more references to anatomy, rooms, babies and mothers.

Normal and Paranormal

Sleep is a normal state, probably an essential period of rest for the entire nervous system, and yet it is also a state in which there is so much paranormal activity that it has always attracted the attention of the psychical researcher.

Alan Angoff

52

SEX AND DREAMS

Sexual dreams have been recorded as far back in history as the Chester Beatty papyrus dating from 1350 B.C. and indicate that sexual dreams were as frequent for Egyptians as for modern day man.

Dr. Robert L. Van de Castle, director of the Sleep and Dream Laboratory of the University of Virginia, with Dr. Calvin Hall analyzed 1,000 dreams of 200 college students. They found that 4 per cent of the women's dreams contained some mention of sex, and 12 per cent of the men's dreams. Women were more likely to report that their dream sexual partners were known to them, whereas the men's dream partners were usually strangers. Petting and kissing were more frequent expressions of sex for the women, intercourse for men.

In a study by Dr. G. V. Hamilton of 200 men and women, 98 per cent of the men said they had had an orgasm in dreams, but only about 40 per cent of the women reported having orgasms, and these occurred usually after marriage (whereas the frequency for men was greater among the singles). Ten to 15 per cent of the men said they had at some time had a sex dream involving their mother, their sisters, or had had homosexual dreams. Women reported homosexual dreams, but very rarely incestual dreams or dreams of sex with animals.

In Kinsey's survey of women, only about 70 per cent reported having had sex dreams at any time. Dream orgasms were reported most frequently by women in their forties — 20 years later than the peak frequency for men. Women's dreams were more likely than men's to add romantic overtones to the sexual activity.

REM and Erections

Erections of the penis almost regularly accompany the REM phase of sleep in adult males, and the duration of the erection is generally coextensive with the duration of the REM period.

A sleep fact

Frequency of Nocturnal Emissions

Kinsey's findings on 5,000 men were that five out of six had had nocturnal emissions at some time in their lives, varying from a dozen a week to once a month. Nocturnal emissions usually began a year or so after the beginning of adolescence and reached their greatest frequency during the late teens and early twenties. Some cases were reported of nocturnal emissions continuing up to age 80.

A sleep fact

ANCIENT DREAM INTERPRETATION

Throughout history the dreams that whirl through heads at night have always given rise to wonder and mystery. In fact, references to dreams and their meanings are found in every culture and in every recorded era of history.

Dream guides that decipher meanings of dreams are on record from as long ago as 500 B.C. in Babylonia and Assyria. Clay tablets with information on interpreting dreams were very common during that period. For example, dreams of flying meant impending disaster. To drink water in a dream meant long life, to drink wine foretold a short one.

The appearance of evil demons in dreams was taken seriously, and various rituals were performed in certain Babylonian temples to solicit help from Mamu, the goddess of dreams.

Serapis was the Egyptian god of dreams, and the famous serapeum temple in Egypt was one of many dedicated to him. Dream interpreters known as Learned Men of the Magic Library had offices in the temples. Dreamers were often sent to temples to sleep and have dreams there.

The ancient Chinese believed that dreams came not from the gods or from demons, but from the dreamer's soul. They believed the soul, called the *hun,* temporarily departed from the body during dreams to communicate with souls of the dead, then returned to the body with special information. An early Chinese book on dreams, the *Meng Shu,* written in the seventh century, also takes astrological factors into account in dream interpretations.

Beyond the Force of Reason

The enigmas in dreams have a close affinity to those things which are signified in an allegoric or hidden sense in the Scriptures. Thus both Joseph and Daniel, through the gift of prophecy, used to interpret dreams, since the force of reason by itself is not powerful enough for getting at truth.

St. Basil the Great

The Mind Alone

And as in a dream we fancy that we hear, and that the organs of hearing are actually impressed, and that we see with our eyes — although neither the bodily organs of sight nor hearing are affected, but it is the mind alone which has these sensations — so there is no absurdity in believing that similar things occurred to the prophets, when it is recorded that they witnessed occurrences of a rather wonderful kind, as when they either heard the words of the Lord or beheld the heavens opened.

Origen

In the Stillness of the Night

Whatever impulse by which the mind of a sleeping person is kept activated and stirring from without, however slight and nominal, has nevertheless a great power to motivate the mind, is firmly grounded in it and cleaves to it tenaciously. This occurs, moreover, because of the stillness of the night, the calm and idleness of the sense organs and the absence of all things to which minds normally direct their attention. For at that time when the senses have been lulled to sleep and the body languishes, what is exterior is not perceived.

Aristotle

The sacred book of India, the *Vedas,* written at least 1,000 years before Christ, stressed the time during the night when a dream occurred as well as its content. Dreams occurring during the first part of the night would not come true for a year, those from the middle period would not come true for eight months, and those from the last part of the night were supposed to be half-realized already.

According to the *Vedas,* it was considered lucky to dream of riding an elephant, unlucky riding a donkey. To dream of losing hair or teeth was viewed as an ill omen. Bad dream predictions, however, could be counteracted by purification rites.

Freud may have been a pioneer in modern thinking about dreams and their relation to the unconscious, but he was far from the first scientist or philosopher to delve into the special world of dreams. And those who think dream interpretation books are popular now should have seen how important they were in the Greek and Roman periods. Socrates, Aristotle, Lucretius, Hippocrates — all spoke often of dreams. Plato believed that dreams expressed the irrational in all of us: "Even in good men, there is a lawless wild-beast nature, which peers out in sleep." There were some 300 temples for interpreting dreams in Greece and the Roman empire, usually dedicated to Aesculapius, god of healing, and containing statues and plaques from visitors whose requests for dreams had been granted.

Hippocrates considered the astrological aspects of dreams important. If in a dream some star appeared dim and above its usual position, for example, difficulties in the head region were suspected. Dreaming of overflowing rivers meant an excess of blood, dreams of springs indicated bladder trouble, dreams of barren trees indicated infertility problems.

Aristotle rejected the divine origin of dreams; nor did he agree with astrological interpretations, as is clear from three books he wrote: *On Dreams; On Sleep and Waking; On Prophecy in Sleep.*

Caesar Augustus once had his life saved by a friend's warning dream and once went about begging alms because he was told to in a dream. Romans were particularly interested in dreams as predictors of the future. They and others often acted on dreams to such an extent, in fact, that dreams have played a key role in many events that have molded world history.

For example, a dream caused Hannibal to make his famous march across the Alps. In his dream a huge serpent moved through a smoke-filled sky with flashes of lightning destroying everything in its path. Then an interpreter appeared in the dream and told Hannibal that the dream represented disasters to befall Italy. When he awoke, Hannibal gave the orders to march.

Another example occurred when Julius Caesar dreamt he was sleeping with his mother, interpreted his mother as symbolizing Rome, and so marched in and captured the city.

Finally, Mohammedan Tàriq ibn-Ziyàd, leader of the Moors, had a dream in which a prophet told him to invade Andalusia. The next morning he began to make plans and so began the Moorish invasion of Spain.

Coincidence? Dreams may have more to do with destinies than people care to believe.

Gengis Khan was told in a dream that he was destined to rule over the Mongols, and in a later dream was told to go and conquer other kingdoms, which he did.

Night Visions

Dreams are of great consequence in the government of the world, of equal authority with the Bible . . . And has not the experience that many men have of significant dreams and night visions a more powerful effect on their minds than the most pure and refined concepts?

David Simpson

Joseph's Dream

Now Joseph had a dream, and when he told it to his brothers they only hated him the more. He said to them, "Hear this dream which I have dreamed: behold, we were binding sheaves in the field, and lo, my sheaf arose and stood upright; and behold, your sheaves gathered round it, and bowed down to my sheaf." His brothers said to him, "Are you indeed to reign over us? Or are you indeed to have dominion over us?" So they hated him yet more for his dreams and for his words.

Genesis 37:5–8

The Upanishads and Sleep

The Mundaka Upanishad asserts that the self has four quarters, namely, the waking state, the dream state, the deep-sleep state, and finally the state of self-realization. The Prasna Upanishad discusses the relationship between the waking state and the sleeping state. The Katha Upanishad asserts that a man can sleep peacefully through the night only when his anger has gone. The Kaushitaki Upanishad shows the relationships between the waking, dream, and sleeping states. It also states that when a man sleeps, speech, hearing, sight, and thought are withdrawn and when he awakes they all reappear.

Gardner Murphy

Primitive Man

To primitive man it seemed as though sleep allowed his spirit to wander from his inert body and to engage in numerous adventures, returning safely to its usual dwelling place at the moment of awakening.

David Foulkes

A dream indirectly affected Adolph Hitler's destiny. In World War I while a soldier in the front lines, he had a dream of warm blood flowing down his chest while he was being buried beneath an avalanche of dirt. Upset by the dream experience, he left his shelter and went for a walk. Within minutes the bunker where he had been was demolished by a direct hit burying alive everyone within it. From that day forward historians say Hitler was convinced he had been spared for some divine mission.

In most primitive cultures dreams are almost as important as real life. For example, if a Cherokee Indian is bitten by a snake in a dream, he is treated for snakebite as though it had really happened. The Cuna Indians who live on islands just off Panama have dream doctors who prescribe various remedies to prevent misfortunes foretold in dreams.

The importance of the dream in primitive cultures has not been sufficiently grasped, says J. S. Lincoln in his book *The Dream in Primitive Culture.* "The primitive mind often assigns a reality value to the fantasy world equal to that of the external world, and even has difficulty at times in distinguishing the two."

Among the Menomini Indian tribe, special ritual puberty dreams are believed to foretell the future of a tribal youth. A Menomini boy or girl was eligible to seek such a dream at age 15 if he or she had never had sexual intercourse. According to custom, they fasted for 8 to 10 days, prayed for a supernatural vision, and expected from the vision guidance for their future life.

Among the Oglala Sioux, if a boy dreamed of a moon with two hands, one holding a bow and arrow and the other a woman's carrying strap, and the boy in the dream ended up with the woman's strap, he was forced to live the rest of his life as a woman, dressing like a woman, doing woman's work, and marrying a man. His only recourse to avoid his fate was suicide.

Perhaps the most famous and important dream book to come from historical times was by Artemidorus, a second-century Italian physician. To prepare for writing the *Dream Book*, he spent his life studying dreams — the dreams of his contemporaries gathered by interviews and from the many practicing dream interpreters, and dreams culled from old manuscripts, including dusty tomes from the Royal Babylonian Library. His dream book was actually five books: three on dream interpretation with facts on 3,000 dreams he had personally collected, and two on how a dream interpreter should conduct himself professionally.

Artemidorus believed there were five different types of dreams: symbolic dreams, daytime visions, oracles of divine revelation, undisguised dreams that dealt with personal concerns in a straightforward way, and nightmares.

He cautioned against mechanically applying his dream interpretation rules and said that the meanings of different symbols could change over time, and with different peoples and cultures. His interpretations were always formulated in relation to the dreamer's background. His six critical questions for interpreting a dream are still valid today:

Were the events of the dream plausible or bizarre?
Were the dream events appropriately inter-connected?
Were the dream events customary for the dreamer?
What pre-dream events may have influenced the dream?
What was the dreamer's occupation?
What was the dreamer's name?

Amazingly Contemporary

Remembering that Artemidorus lived in the Second Century, his insights into the complexities that must be considered in deducing the meaning of a particular dream are amazingly compatible with contemporary dynamic approaches.

Dr. Robert L. Van de Castle

A Fourth-Century Theologian's View

Most men's dreams are conformed to the state of their character: the brave man's fancies are of one kind, the coward's of another; the wanton man's dreams of one kind, the continent man's of another; the liberal man and the avaricious man are subject to different fancies; while these fancies are nowhere framed by the intellect, but by the less rational disposition of the soul, which forms even in dreams the semblances of those things to which each is accustomed by the practice of his waking hours.

Gregory of Nyssa

DREAMS AND RELIGION

Some of the world's religions owe their origin and development to dreams.

In a dream Mohammed was given the mission of founding Mohammedanism. In fact, over a six-months period of intense dreaming, he was given the minutest details about what the format of the new religion should be. Most of the Koran was revealed to him through dreams. Dreams were so important to Mohammed that he and his disciples met every morning to report their dreams for interpretation. The *Tabqat al-Mu'abbirin,* an Arabian dream book published in the eleventh century, contains names of 7,000 dream interpreters!

The Babylonian Talmud contains four chapters on dreams.

Buddha's coming was announced symbolically in a dream which his mother, Queen Maya, had of a beautiful elephant. The interpretation was that she would give birth to a son who would become a universal monarch.

Christianity began with Gabriel appearing to Mary in a vision, telling her she was to become the mother of Christ. According to the gospel of Matthew, Joseph received divine commands in four different dreams; in one he was told to name the child, Jesus. A few centuries later the Emperor Constantine had a dream which inspired him to impose Christianity on his empire.

There are some 70 dreams and visions mentioned in the Bible. Probably the most famous is Pharaoh's dream of the seven fat and seven lean kine as meaning seven years of plenty followed by seven years of famine.

Ladder To Heaven

Taking one of the stones of the place, Jacob put it under his head and lay down in that place to sleep. And he dreamed that there was a ladder set up on the earth, and the top of it reached to heaven; and behold, the angels of God were ascending and descending on it! And behold, the Lord stood above it and said, "I am the Lord, the God of Abraham your father and the God of Isaac; the land on which you lie I will give to you and to your descendants; and your descendants shall be like the dust of the earth, and you shall spread abroad to the west and to the east and to the north and to the south; and by you and your descendants shall all the families of the earth bless themselves. Behold, I am with you and will keep you wherever you go, and will bring you back to this land; for I will not leave you until I have done that of which I have spoken to you." Then Jacob awoke from his sleep and said, "Surely the Lord is in this place; and I did not know it."

Genesis 28:11–16

Our Silent Counselor

Let us all deliver ourselves to the interpretation of dreams, men and women, young and old. . . . Sleep offers itself to all: it is an oracle always ready, to our infallible and silent counselor.
Synesius of Cyrene
Bishop, 5th Century

Don't Tell Me

Don't tell me what you dreamt last night,
for I've been reading Freud.

Franklin P. Adams

According to Dr. Robert L. Van de Castle in *Psychology of Dreaming*, with the growth of Christianity, dreams gradually came to be linked with sin, sex and demons.

"The dream was something to be avoided as it allowed a portal of easy access for the devil whereby he could sway men's minds in evil directions," writes Van de Castle. "Under the Church Fathers, the dream fell from its previously exalted position to one of despisement, and the dream is still devaluated by many contemporary theologians."

Two Church Fathers, Saint Augustine and Gregory of Nyssa, both spoke of passions in dreams. From dreams it could be determined whether a person was lustful or chaste.

In the thirteenth century St. Thomas Aquinas spoke of dreams caused by physical factors as well as arising from God or demons.

In medieval times, if the devil appeared frequently in a person's dreams, the dreamer could be suspected of being in allegiance with him and might be burned at the stake. Witness many paintings from the Dark Ages that depict leering, hideous creatures populating the dream scene of some hapless victim.

Martin Luther was so afraid of his dreams — that he would not be able to distinguish divine from demonic messages — he prayed to God not to speak to him in his dreams.

A Work of Devils

Incubi or Succubi punish men in the night . . . For Satan himself transforms himself into various shapes and forms; and by seducing in dreams the mind, which he holds captive, leads it . . .

The apparitions that come in dreams proceed . . . of an intrinsic local motion in the head and cells of the brain. And this can also happen through a similar local motion created by devils.

Malleus Maleficarum

Distinguishing Illusions and Revelations

Saints at times distinguish between illusions and revelations, the real voices and images of visions, with penetrating delicacy, so that they know what they may receive from good inspiration and what they may suffer from illusion. For if the mind of man, which does occasionally utter many truths that it might serve in the end to free the soul from some misconception, were not alerted against these things, it would plunge itself through the agency of the deceiving spirit into many futile pursuits.

St. Gregory

CONTEMPORARY DREAM ANALYSTS

Sigmund Freud. The interpretation of dreams was an important part of Sigmund Freud's technique for uncovering unconscious psychological problems that lay at the root of a patient's symptoms. In fact, he discussed dreams in 26 different books and articles, his major treatise being *The Interpretation of Dreams.* Published in 1899, only 351 copies were sold after six years. Freud wrote in the preface of his final edition in 1932, "This book, with the new contribution to psychology which surprised the world when it was published, remains essentially unaltered. It contains, even according to my present-day judgment, the most valuable of all the discoveries it has been my good fortune to make. Insight such as this falls to one's lot but once in a lifetime."

Freud believed there were two levels to dreams: One was the actual narrative of what happened, which he called the *manifest content.* The *manifest content,* he believed, had no significance, but was only a disguise for repressed drives and emotional conflicts underlying the dream which he called the *latent content.* He felt dreams were the guardians of these hidden wishes and desires, and were disguised thus to protect us from such unconscious drives.

Everything Is the Dreamer

This is the real nature of the dream. It reflects some kernel of reflection on one's life. It represents this visually as a scene and events. Everything in the scene is the dreamer. The most conscious feelings of the dreamer are his in the dream. Less conscious aspects are represented by others. The more alien the others are (i.e., different in age, race, disposition) the more alien are those aspects of the self. Even the objects in the dream are parts of the self.... Everything in the dream is fashioned out of the life of the individual and it reflects that life. What he can't recognize in that life looks "other" to him in the dream too. But of course that is how we all live! Neither in the dream nor in life do we recognize all the selves with which we have peopled our environment.

Wilson Van Dusen

According to Freud, the sleeping brain acted as a censor, presenting thoughts to us through dreams in ways that would be acceptable. His emphasis was on the dream drawing from past experience, usually from childhood. A dream's motivating force was wish fulfillment, he felt, and every dream was a wish from the unconscious, almost always having a sexual basis. Four kinds of wishes he enumerated were (1) those consciously remembered that were aroused during the day but left unfulfilled, (2) wishes that arose during the day but were unacceptable and repressed into the unconscious, (3) wishes that arose during the night stimulated by hunger or the need to urinate, and (4) wishes originating in the unconscious that were incapable of *ever* passing censorship into the conscious. He emphatically rejected the idea that the dream could involve normal thinking processes.

Freud had a long list of symbols signifying sexual organs or sexual wishes. In his own words:

"All elongated objects, such as sticks, tree trunks and umbrellas (the opening of these last being comparable to an erection) may stand for the male organ — as well as all long, sharp weapons, such as knives, daggers and pikes. . . . Boxes, cases, chests, cupboards and ovens represent the uterus, and also hollow objects, ships, and vessels of all kinds. Rooms in dreams are usually women; if the various ways in and out of them are represented, this interpretation is scarcely open to doubt. . . . A dream of going through a suite of rooms is a brothel or harem dream. . . . Steps, ladders or staircases, or, as the case may be, walking up or down them, are representations of the sexual act. Smooth walls over which the dreamer climbs, the façades of houses . . . correspond to erect human bodies, and are probably repeating in the dream recollections of a baby's climbing up his parents or nurse. . . . 'Wood' seems, from its linguistic connections, to stand in general

The Inner World

The dream may be considered as the window of one's inner world. The internal dialogues of the dream center around basic questions of our life—who we are, our attitude to our creative work, and our feelings to others and to ourselves. When we are actively involved in our dreams, opportunities for greater awareness occur. With constructive reflection, breaking out of old patterns of behavior, into expanding new ones will lead to new integrations of personality.

Dr. Harry Gershman

for female 'material'. . . . A woman's hat can very often be interpreted with certainty as a genital organ, and, moreover, as a *man's*. The same is true of an overcoat. . . . In men's dreams a neck-tie often appears as a symbol for the penis. . . . It is highly probable that all complicated machinery and apparatus occurring in dreams stand for the genitals (and as a rule male ones). . . . Nor is there any doubt that all weapons and tools are used as symbols for the male organ: e.g., ploughs, hammers, rifles, revolvers, daggers, sabres, etc. In the same way many landscapes in dreams, especially any containing bridges or wooded hills, may clearly be recognised as descriptions of the genitals. . . . Children in dreams often stand for genitals. . . . Playing with a little child, beating it, etc., often represent masturbation in dreams. To represent castration symbolically, the dream-work makes use of baldness, hair-cutting, falling out of teeth and decapitation. If one of the ordinary symbols for a penis occurs in a dream doubled or multiplied, it is to be regarded as a warding-off of castration. The appearance in dreams of lizards — animals whose tails grow again if they are pulled off — has the same significance. . . . The genitals can also be represented in dreams by other parts of the body: the male organ by a hand or a foot and the female genital orifice by the mouth or an ear or even an eye."

Jung, Stekel and Others Carl Jung, a Swiss psychiatrist, was born in 1875, just 19 years after Freud. His first book, *The Psychology of the Unconscious*, criticized Freud's emphasis on sexuality and led to a split between them.

Dreams were also important to Jung and he once estimated that over the years as a psychiatrist he had listened to some 80,000 dreams. Rather than viewing the dream as a protective guardian, Jung considered it as a means to alert the dreamer to some hidden facets about himself. For Jung, dreams acted to

Language of Dreams

It must be made perfectly clear, however, that these symbols can *never* be studied from a book to give an easy, shorthand method of understanding dreams. Like any living language, they must be read in context, in connection with the personal associations they hold for the dreamer.

Morton T. Kelsey

A Warning Dream

And when they departed, behold, the angel of the Lord appeared to Joseph in a dream, saying, "Arise, and take the young child and his mother and flee into Egypt."

Matthew 11:13

Behind All Dreams

Nature is the one and the same force behind all dreams; thus, there ought to be a constant criterion for believing either in all dreams or in none. But in most dreams it is not possible to believe; therefore, there is no reason why, when most dreams have been discredited, we ought to believe in any in particular. In addition, if certain dreams are trustworthy and definite, it is necessary that there be some definite efficient cause of them. But what are the causes? Nature, people say, and God. Yet nature, indeed, is a friend of order and constancy; and in dreams there is no order, but inconstancy full of accident. Moreover, it seems beneath God and foreign to his majesty, that He should approach the couches of sleeping men, rush to their bedsides and interrupt their snoring with dreams which they would not remember, not understand, or even contemn upon awakening.

Xenophanes
and the Epicureans

correct any one-sided development of personality. They would show the dreamer in what directions he should move to correct any problems. He felt that dreams were generally oriented toward the future, rather than to the past as Freud thought.

Jung believed there were symbols in dreams, but he did not believe they stood for anything that already existed; rather they represented something not yet recognized or formulated.

He felt some dreams were *archetypes,* that is, they represented expressions of mankind's collective unconscious that had evolved through human history at a very deep unconscious level.

Another psychoanalyst with a deep interest in dreams was Wilhelm Stekel, who also broke off from Freud and formulated a concept called *active analytic therapy*. He felt that the kinds of dreams and interpretations brought to analysts by their patients often reflect the psychoanalyst's theories not because of their intrinsic validity but because the patient is trying to fit his dreams to the analyst's theories. Stekel emphasized brief treatment of patients, having them keep a daily diary of their dreams. He thought the first dream reported was especially important.

Emil Gutheil, one of Stekel's students, also emphasized the danger of the suggestive role played by therapists in dream analysis.

Psychotherapist Medard Boss estimates that he has been told some 50,000 dreams by patients in his 25 years of practice. He believes in concentrating on the dream itself, foregoing theories and hypotheses of the past since the actual contents of the dream often reveal the person's thoughts quite directly and fully.

Serious students of the theories of dream analysis are referred to *The World of Dreams* by Ralph Woods, an anthology citing excerpts from the works of 214 authors on dreams.

ESP AND DREAMS

Presidents Lincoln and Kennedy both are reported to have dreamed of their deaths shortly before their assassinations. There have been many reports of persons dreaming of impending disasters; in fact, a special center has been set up to collect and study such reports. Soviet scientists report after a 28-year study that dreams often reveal the nature of an illness long before the doctor has enough evidence to make a diagnosis.

How valid are these reports? How much truth is there in the link between extra-sensory perception and dreams?

A number of sleep and dream laboratories are trying to investigate this aspect of dreams on a scientific level. Much of the research is being carried on in the Dream Laboratory of Maimonides Hospital in Brooklyn, New York, where researchers are studying precognition and clairvoyance.

Some experiments there test whether the thoughts of one person can affect the dreams of another. Dr. Stanley Krippner, director of the laboratory, and Dr. Montague Ullman, chief of psychiatry at the hospital, are probably best known in scientific circles for the experiments in which one person sits isolated in a room and concentrates on a target object such as a painting, and tries to transmit that picture to a person sleeping in a laboratory down the hall. Strict surveillance is kept and the paintings are selected by random means from sealed envelopes after the receiving subject is sound asleep.

The transference of thoughts does not always work, and better results are obtained with some people than others, but there have been enough direct hits to make the most critical skeptic stop and wonder. For example, in one instance the target object was a

Why Miss Napier?

On Thursday night of last week, being at the office here, I dreamed that I saw a lady in a red shawl with her back towards me *(whom I supposed to be E.)*. On her turning round I found that I didn't know her and she said, "I am Miss Napier." All the time I was dressing next morning, I thought—what a preposterous thing to have so very distinct a dream about nothing! And why Miss Napier? For I never heard of any Miss Napier. That same Friday night I read. After the reading, came into my retiring-room Miss Boyle and her brother, and *the* Lady in the red shawl whom they present as "Miss Napier"!

These are all the circumstances exactly told.

Charles Dickens

Dreams Are Revelations

There have been epochs in the history of Western civilization in which dreams have been treated with great reverence, as signs and portents of a spirit world or as messages from heavenly powers. There have been other periods in which dreams have been regarded as idle sputterings of the brain, meaningless bits of mental fluff to which only fools would pay attention. In our own era, under the influence of psychoanalytic theory, dreams are regarded as revelations, not of the divine, but of our own inner selves.

David Foulkes

Gauguin painting, "The Moon and the Earth," showing a nude Tahitian girl. The subject being tested — a secretary — dreamed of wearing a bathing suit, later of a girl trying to get a tan.

Another Gauguin was used, a still life of three puppies and blue goblets. The volunteer dreamed of "a couple of dogs making noise" and saw "dark blue bottles."

In general, when telepathy is successful the receivers respond in one of four ways to the pictures sent: They describe the general outline of the object involved, they pick up one corner or detail, they receive the mood or color or emotional content of the painting, or they make an association with some object, such as changing an airplane to a dirigible or substituting one animal for another.

Subjects may be secretaries, models, cabdrivers, or the scientists or their assistants. When one cab-driver was tested, he dreamed "something about posts . . . about Madison Square Garden and a boxing match." The sender had been concentrating on "Dempsey and Firpo," a painting of two boxers at Madison Square Garden.

One of the most successful receivers so far is Dr. William Erwin, a New York psychologist. When the painting was Van Gogh's "Boats on the Beach," he reported "being on a boardwalk or the beach . . . the sea coast . . . it makes me think of Van Gogh perhaps." When the painting being sent was "The Sacrament of the Last Supper," he had a series of dreams. They involved a table, the ocean, a glass of wine, a magician, a group of people in which one was trying to do something destructive, fishing boats, fishermen, Christmas, a doctor, a psychiatrist, the Mediterranean area, biblical times, food and a restaurant.

Some subjects dreamed of the pictures even when these remained sealed in the envelopes throughout the experiment.

Native Nudity

The dream becomes a revelation. It strips the ego of its artificial wrappings and exposes it in its native nudity. It brings up from the dim depths of our conscious life the primal, instinctive impulses, and discloses to us a side of ourselves which connects us with the great sentient world.

James Sully

Dreams are Prophets

If dreams are prophets, and if the visions seen in dreams are riddles of their future fortunes to anxious men, they would in that case be full of wisdom, though certainly not clear. In sooth their lack of clearness is their wisdom. "For the gods keep man's life concealed."

Synesius of Cyrene

Occasionally, accidentally, the dreamer will pick up thoughts in the laboratory not connected with the target painting. One night a sender glanced through a copy of *Life* magazine and got caught up in an intriguing photo story about topless swimsuits. The dreamer dreamed of statue busts of two women.

One subject dreamed of a high school friend he hadn't seen in 20 years. Later, while sitting in a restaurant telling someone about the dream, he saw the old friend standing in line. Coincidence or precognition in the dream?

An interesting finding made at the lab was that the most productive ESP dreams were those occurring when just falling asleep (hypnagogic) or when just awakening (hypnopompic). Those stages of drifting imagery are made up mostly of alpha waves which have been found to be particularly sensitive to high ESP activity. Drs. Krippner and Ullman also found that the dream response is higher when the image being sent is a vivid one, and when two friends work together. The image is further reinforced when the sender also concentrates on related objects, uses correlated music or scents, or performs some activity related to the painting being sent.

A number of psychiatrists report that they often encounter telepathy in analysis, says Dr. Ullman. "Many persons can communicate at a telepathic level and surprise the therapist with a telepathic dream of rich awareness even of the physician's problems." One of his own patients dreamt that Ullman was making a speech to a large crowd in a foreign language that no one understood. This happened at a time when Ullman was feeling anxious about an upcoming speech because he wasn't sure that he could make the audience understand the complexities of the topic.

So the dreams people dream may possibly be thoughts sent by somebody else.

Visitations In Sleep

I speak of visitations in sleep, such as the apparition to Joseph in a dream, in the manner experienced in most cases of the kind. In the same manner, therefore, our own friends also who have departed this life before us sometimes come and appear to us in dreams, and speak to us. For I myself remember that Profuturus, and Privatus, and Servilius, holy men who within my recollection were removed by death from our monastery, spoke to me, and that the events of which they spoke came to pass according to their words. Or if it be some other higher spirit that assumes their form and visits our minds, I leave this to the all-seeing eye of Him before whom everything from the highest to the lowest is uncovered. If, therefore, the Lord be pleased to speak through reason to your Holiness on all these questions, I beg you to be so kind as make me partaker of the knowledge which you have received.

Evodius Bishop of Uzala
A letter to St. Augustine

USING AND MISUSING
SLEEP TIME

SLEEP NEEDS

Sleep can be one of the most pleasant parts of a full human life, but few people take advantage of its potential benefits and pleasures.

Some people need practical suggestions to help them take real advantage of their sleep and dream time. They want to prepare a rewarding sleep environment for themselves both within the self and in the external surroundings. Others will seek to understand how to use dreams and sleep to their own advantage and enhancement. Still others wish to probe the problems of insomnia, sleepwalking, nightmares and other sleep difficulties and look for ways to solve them. Everyone wants to obtain the most benefits physically and emotionally from sleeping time.

The first question people ask is, "*How much sleep does a person really need?*"

According to research and experience, the amount of sleep people need varies tremendously. There is no "normal" amount. Different people sleep different lengths of time. A person will sleep longer one night than another. And people have different sleep patterns at different ages.

Advice from the 17th Century

Five hours sleep a traveller, seven a scholar, eight a merchant, and eleven every knave.

Torriano

Why Humans Must Sleep

Many different theories of sleep have attempted to explain its recurrence and apparent necessity. Some stress nervous fatigue or exhaustion; others, the accumulation of metabolic waste products in brain or body; still others, hormone accumulation and discharge. In spite of the fact that much is now known about the mechanisms immediately responsible for the onset and maintenance of sleep, it is still unclear why humans must sleep and why they need as much as they do.

David Foulkes

Although a person may sleep longer one night than another, depending on circumstances — season, caffeine intake and so forth — the number of hours an individual sleeps over a week's time or a month's time averages out incredibly accurately. The average of one week usually falls within one-half hour's amount of each other week. Eventually people make up lost sleep in accordance with their particular individual patterns. However, all sleep experts agree that the more regular the sleep hours, the better and more beneficial the sleep.

How much sleep people need depends on metabolism as well as weather, season, health, kind of work, and the amount of present stress.

Some doctors believe that individuals are born with certain basic sleep needs and should not try to change their inner biological rhythms. Eight hours a night is the usual quoted average, but surveys show that a good night's sleep ranges from less than five hours a night to more than ten. Time needed for adequate sleep changes with age, as does the quality of sleep. The older person often sleeps more, but enjoys it less.

Some fall asleep quickly and deeply. Gradually, toward morning, their sleep becomes lighter and they awaken by themselves. Others take a long while to fall asleep initially but once they touch bottom they stay there. With them, sleep deepens as morning draws on so that it's an ordeal to wake up.

The biggest changes in patterns of sleep amounts occur with age. Newborn infants sleep an average of $16\frac{1}{2}$ hours daily. Gradually the baby begins to give up some sleeping time and by the 26th week of life usually averages about 14 hours. Also by this time the baby is doing about three-fourths of his sleeping at night.

From ages 2 through 19, less and less time is spent in sleep. At age 2 the average sleep time is 12½ hours; 1½ hours of nap time and 11 hours at night. Again the average operates within wide variations. By age 6 most children have given up their nap and sleep time is reduced to about 11 hours. Sleep time of the 10-year-old averages 10 hours. By age 15 it has dropped to about 9 hours. From ages 15 to 19 it averages around 8½ to 8¾ hours every night. Interestingly, comparative studies show that American children sleep from one to one and a half hours longer than German or English children.

As a person enters old age his total daily sleep time again becomes longer. Some people are day-people, some people are night-people, some are completely flexible, apparently having more control over their sleep and waking.

People can come to know their own bodies and learn their own sleep needs. They can find out how flexible or deeply patterned they are. They can then follow the pattern that suits them physically and emotionally.

Need a lot of sleep? One doctor says, "Go ahead and sleep for half your life — you'll enjoy the other half twice as much."

Whether people are short sleepers or long sleepers, their dream time seems to adjust. It has been found that short sleepers — 6 hours or less — put in about the same number of hours of Stage 4 and REM sleep as the average sleeper of 7½ hours. Naturally, for the short sleeper there is less time spent in light sleep and awakening. Perhaps long sleepers — those sleeping over 9 hours — are simply poorer sleepers and the short sleepers are more "efficient" sleepers. Or, perhaps, by improving the quality of sleep the body does not need as much quantity.

Amounts of Sleep

The variations in amount of sleep taken by a child from day to day were large; . . . the variations in weekly, biweekly, or triweekly averages for the same child were surprisingly small.

Dr. M. M. Reynolds

Sleep and Mental Performance

In loss of sleep a higher level of physical effort is required to maintain mental performance (a conclusion easily concurred in by the tired reader who at the end of the day is fighting to keep his eyelids up and his mind open). The human subject can be kept awake for periods up to 120 hours, but after 48 hours, according to Kleitman, the subject is sleep-bound, requires a lot of stimulation to produce a response, and is not much good.

Annals of Internal Medicine

DREAM QUOTAS

Do Animals Dream?

Do animals dream? Anyone who has ever watched a dog sleep has never doubted it as he trembles, jerks, and whines in what appears to be a great rabbit chase. Scientists say that they have recorded patterns from animals indicating dream stages of sleep.

A sleep fact

Convincing Dreams

So convincing were these dreams of lying awake that he awoke from them each morning in complete exhaustion and fell right back to sleep.

Joseph Heller
Catch 22

Sleeptalking

When a person talks in his sleep, it usually relates to what he is dreaming. The sleeptalker can also hear what someone in the awake world says, often incorporating it into his dream and answering the outsider. Sleeptalkers almost never remember talking in their sleep even if you wake them up immediately after the episode.

Scientists find that disconnected and incoherent sleeptalking usually occurs in deep sleep: talk of a more intelligent pattern arises during REM.

A sleep fact

Amount of sleep time is important, but so is the amount of dream time.

Scientists determined this after using EEGs to study sleep and dreams. By watching the EEGs, they could tell when sleepers started dreaming. By waking subjects each time during the first moments of a dream, they were able to prevent the sleepers from dreaming. Result: Subjects became anxious and irritable, and their anxiety increased with each night of dream deprivation.

Dr. W. C. Dement is responsible for much of this experimentation. He found that volunteers after four or five nights of dream deprivation seemed anxious, irritable and quite unable to concentrate. After two weeks they manifested definite personality changes and one subject became paranoid.

When Dr. Dement was able to reduce dreaming in a subject by 65 to 75 per cent, he found that on the following nights the subject's REM sleep — dreaming sleep — set in sooner and lasted much longer, consuming a greater percentage of total sleep time than normally. The person was making up for lost dream time!

One researcher, Dr. Ernest Hartmann of Boston, believes that dream time is connected to some premenstrual tension symptoms. He speculates that because of hormone changes women need extra dream time during premenstrual periods. (Women, in fact, dream more as they near menstrual periods.) Dr. Hartmann feels some of the irritability and fatigue characteristic of the premenstrual blues may be due to an unsatisfied need for dreaming, and he recommends more sleep time and thus more dream time during this period as a way to help alleviate symptoms of premenstrual tension.

BEAUTY SLEEP

Sleep — deep, sound, untroubled sleep — is one of the best beauty aids in the world. When people don't get enough sleep they look haggard, bleary-eyed, gray. Why? What makes the difference? Part of the reason is that sleep really is a time of physical repair and renewal.

The cells of the body are continuously dying and being replaced, and much of that replacement occurs during sleep. According to some research, skin cells divide and make new cells about twice as fast while a person sleeps as they do when he's awake. In fact, next to proper nourishment, adequate sleep is probably the biggest factor in helping people look younger longer.

In addition, during sleep the body gets rid of skin waste products and circulates in the skin certain essential ingredients such as minerals, vitamins, hormones. When people cut down on sleep they cut down the circulation of these elements and contract the capillaries. Without necessary sleep, skin is deprived of normal solutions that usually bathe and refresh it at night. Consequently, skin tissues sink and sag, and collagen — a dark protein in the tissues — becomes increasingly visible. Visible collagen accounts for dark circles under people's eyes. Other skin tissues hold waste fluids which cause morning puffiness. Usually, a good sleep can restore such skin, but if a person goes without rest long enough, this skin condition may become irreversible.

How We View Sleep

Sleep is a personal matter. How we view our sleep is a function of how we view life in general. If it's an especially difficult day ahead of us, we think we have not slept enough. But if it's an exciting and rewarding thing we're looking forward to, we think we are done with sleep . . . There are many people who abhor the moment to sleep and are delighted to waken to face the next day. Others seek sleep as a refuge and an escape. How we view sleep tells us something about ourselves, more, perhaps, than we had ever thought possible.

Dr. Julius Segal

Healthy, Wealthy and Wise

Early to bed,
and early to rise,
makes a man healthy, wealthy,
and wise.

Benjamin Franklin

Gathering Strength

There are pauses amidst study, and even pauses of seeming idleness, in which a process goes on which may be likened to the digestion of food. In those seasons of repose, the powers are gathering their strength for new efforts; as land which lies fallow recovers itself for tillage.

J. W. Alexander

An Ability to Sleep

**Sleeping time of a species of animal
seems to be related to its lifespan. Both
bats and shrews, for example, are small,
very active and have very high metabolism rates. The bat sleeps up to 20
hours a day, the shrew is busy, busy,
busy, and seldom sleeps. The shrew lives
about two years, the bat 18. Scientists
think the difference is due to the bat's
ability to sleep.**

A sleep fact

CHEATING ON SLEEP TIME

Sleep is such an essential human need that to sacrifice sleep time is to imperil both body and mind.

A human being can survive food starvation for three weeks, but deprived of sleep continuously for three weeks he will disintegrate mentally and may even become psychotic. Frequent sleep-cheating can take its toll, too.

Dr. Julius Segal, scientist at the National Institute of Mental Health and expert on sleep, declares that danger lurks in chronic sleep loss — the day-by-day building up of small sleep losses until the cumulative loss brings about strong harmful effects.

Chronically cheating yourself of sleep, he says, can cause the following conditions: Lapse of attention, inability to respond to critical information, slow thinking, indecision, impaired memory, withdrawal, erratic behavior, weakening of ethical standards, irritability and unpredictable rages.

82

Why do people give up sleep?

Sometimes out of sheer necessity — for example, to complete a job that must be done. But, says Dr. Segal in *Internal Medicine News,* "Many among us regard their inadequate sleep with a touch of triumph. These are persons for whom sleeplessness has become something of a status symbol. If you are sincere and worry about life the way you're 'supposed' to, they would argue, then you must naturally suffer from insomnia. It's a badge of success — like ulcers or coronaries."

"The social waste, the expense, error, and needless tragedy evolving from lost sleep is unnecessary," he continues. "We have seen how judgment fades, how strong ethical purposes can diminish, how mental functions decline, and finally transient psychotic symptoms can begin to dominate the rational man. Neither society nor the individual can afford these incursions."

The tempo of American life continues to quicken. People push themselves to the limit, use up their own natural energies, and then turn to the artificial stimulation of drugs, just to keep going. Like the reckless gamblers already playing with borrowed money, fatigued sleepless Americans begin living in the red, using the artificial energies offered by well-advertised drugs.

There are differences in sleep needs, of course, and people experience different needs at different times, but the danger lies in the chronic, constant loss of sleep. It's important that people know what their limits are and not exceed them.

A few presidents may have couches in their offices for taking periodic rests, but most personnel, even in crucial jobs, are forced to keep going all day no matter how fatigued they may be. People who can find a place to stretch out for ten minutes during the day are encouraged to do so; a sleep break instead of a coffee break is a good way to get back to peak efficiency.

Sleep Deprivation

Experimenters who have deliberately sleep-deprived animals report that the animals may actually die after ten or more sleepless days, and there is sometimes an indication in post-mortem analyses that such sleep deprivation has produced degeneration in the tissue of the brain and other bodily organs.

A sleep fact

Sleep Starvation

The effects of sleep starvation have altered the course of human events, but civilized society has remained quite cavalier about the need for sleep. We live in a world that relies upon split-second reactions — from automobile drivers, pilots, operators of machines — and that demands rapid business decisions involving high stakes. The demands for speed and judgment count upon the performance of a sane and rested man, but there is slight provision for rest. Nowhere does one see beds. Not in the newest office buildings of major cities do the rest rooms actually provide dormitories where people might sleep.

Dr. Julius Segal

The Least Rested

The study of sleep loss may have many social implications. The world might, indeed, be different if everyone got nine hours' sleep, and if key decision makers were not among the least rested members of society.

Gay Gaer Luce

A Need for Sleep

How many thousand of my poorest
    subjects
Are at this hour asleep? O sleep,
    O gentle sleep,
Nature's soft nurse, how have I frighted
    thee,
That thou no more wilt weigh my
    eyelids down
And steep my senses in forgetfulness?

Shakespeare
Henry IV

Elephants are Night-owls

Do elephants sleep long? No. Elephants are nightowls. They go to bed late — usually after midnight — and generally sleep only two or three hours.

A sleep fact

Biological time clocks or not, regular sleep schedules or not, sometimes a person has to get that paper done, finish a report, rewrite that story, or meet tomorrow's deadline. He simply has to stay up all night, or most of it. What does he do?

First, he should eat a high-protein dinner. Protein gives more staying power. Later on, a snack of bouillon or orange juice will prove more helpful than a cup of coffee. Sometimes coffee creates jumpiness and hinders concentration. Those who can manage it should squeeze in a three-hour nap when the system begins to fall apart; then wake up and hit the project again during the early morning hours.

Those who are forced to lose sleep over several nights working on a project, as well as putting in work hours during the day, should try taking naps during the day or night, whenever the brain begins to turn off.

It's helpful to vary the environment: first work at a desk, then on the bed, then at the dining room table. Work with music, then without. Walk around the room a bit. Do five minutes of exercises every hour or two. Some people wash their face first with hot water, then with ice cold. They also brush their teeth and comb their hair. Anything to freshen the body.

Midnight oil-burners who have had the same clothes on most of the day and night can change into pajamas or other lounge clothes to give the body a different feel.

Open a window for awhile. Avoid people who tell you that you really should stop and get some rest. All-night workers need to be left alone by people like that.

Surround yourself with food. Eat and drink. Eat and drink. Eat and drink. Use every maneuver to freshen the body and keep the mind attentive.

TO SLEEP, PERCHANCE TO LEARN

Once, on his television program, Art Linkletter offered to test sleep learning by trying to learn Mandarin Chinese — reportedly the most difficult language in the world. He listened to recordings for ten nights, then, on his television show, he conversed in Chinese with the vice consul of China.

How valid is sleep learning? Can the brain absorb information from a recorded message tucked under a pillow at night? Is it possible to change a habit, to memorize, to learn a language during sleep?

In theory, sleep learning should work. It is well known that the sleeping brain is active and that the sleeper can receive messages from the outside world. But aside from these few facts, there has been surprisingly little research on sleep learning and results of testing seem ambiguous.

The most productive experiments were probably those of Drs. C. Michael Levy and Wilse B. Webb of the University of Florida. To test sleep learning they played tape recorded messages of Russian and English nouns to students who had no prior knowledge of Russian. Students were able to retain up to about 30 per cent of the material, the doctors said.

One tape was played twice, another three times, with a message such as: "This is your Russian teacher. You are asleep and relaxed; you hear my voice and you will not wake up. You will remember these words and their meanings forever."

Ten Billion Nerve Cells

A brain contains more than ten billion nerve cells each of which averages about ten thousand connections with others; each cell, in turn, contains at a minimum ten thousand complex macromolecules, not only in constant agitation but being renewed about ten thousand times in a lifespan. Thus, looking at it from the worm's-eye view of the macromolecule, brain action must deal in a lifetime with at least 10^{22} (10,000,000,000,000,000,000,000) macromolecular constellations in various degrees of instability and impermanence.

Dr. P. Weiss

REM Dreams and Learning

Dreams during the REM period seem to be related to learning in some way. Humans in infancy, learning more intensely than at any other period of life, spend 50 per cent of their sleep in REM, compared with 20 per cent for adults. Persons who have had a brain injury and need to relearn a great deal of material also have increased REM sleep.

A sleep fact

Symbols to Open the World

The unconscious activity of modern man ceaselessly presents him with innumerable symbols, and each of them has a particular message to transmit, a particular mission to accomplish, in order to ensure or to reestablish the equilibrium of the psyche. As we have seen, the symbol not only makes the world "open" but also helps religious man to attain to the universal. For it is through symbols that man finds his way out of his particular situation and "opens himself" to the general and the universal. Symbols awaken individual experience and transmute it into a spiritual act, into metaphysical comprehension of the world.

Mircea Eliade

Scores over five nights indicated that sleep learning ability improves with practice. It also indicated that students seemed to learn better in a light sleep, particularly a light sleep late in the night.

The doctors believe that sleep learning will work especially well with hypnotically suggestible individuals. And they feel that although new learning is probably best accomplished while awake, long-term retention of facts may best be achieved by intensive repetition during sleep.

Probably the most extensive experiment in sleep learning was undertaken in the Soviet Union. There in a town called Dubna, home of the Joint Institute of Nuclear Research, some 1,000 residents tried to learn English by radio in their sleep. Results of the test are not known.

Experiments at the Ukranian Academy of Sciences in Kiev, which has been trying to develop methods of sleep learning, show that the most effective teaching period is during the 15 to 30 minutes before the student falls asleep, and in the first 20 to 30 minutes of sleep that follow, in contrast to American research evidence that sleep learning works best in late light sleep.

Both American and Russian tests indicate that little information can be absorbed while in deep stages of sleep.

At this point in research, most scientists and educators do not recommend sleep learning as a practical way to learn. They feel that although learning can take place during periods of semi-wakefulness or light sleep, these are times of low mental acuity so that whatever learning might occur would not be of significant value.

At present, most educators suggest that the best method for learning is to study while awake and then get a good night's sleep.

MAKING BEDTIME EASY FOR CHILDREN

Going to bed is a special time for children. It can be a time of warmth and security and love, a satisfying ending to a good day; or it can be a time of tears or fear, generating a feeling of being cut off from parents and familiar things. How a child is put to bed can determine which it will be.

Here are six guidelines for making bedtime easy and pleasant for parents *and* children.

1. *Put yourself in the child's place.* How would you like to be right in the middle of relaxing or in the middle of an absorbing task when someone barges in, points a finger, and screams get-ready-for-bed-this-instant - it's - five - minutes - past - your - bedtime - I - don't-want-to-hear-a-word-from-you-just-go!

A little respect for the child's feelings will be helpful, and even though firmness is sometimes necessary it can be combined with warmth and love, and with some advance notice.

2. *Establish a bedtime routine.* Children love the security of the known and the familiar. Let washing, brushing teeth, picking up toys, getting into pajamas be done at a regular time and become expected routine; this avoids hassle over every step. It can also help sometimes — if the child enjoys it — to have bedtime preparation early in the evening, with time left over for snacks, games, or reading.

My Bed Is a Boat

My bed is like a little boat;
　Nurse helps me in when I embark;
She girds me in my sailor's coat
　And starts me in the dark.

At night, I go on board and say
　Good night to all my friends on shore;
I shut my eyes and sail away
　And see and hear no more.

And sometimes things to bed I take,
　As prudent sailors have to do:
Perhaps a slice of wedding-cake,
　Perhaps a toy or two.

All night across the dark we steer:
　But when the day returns at last,
Safe in my room, beside the pier,
　I find my vessel fast.

Robert Louis Stevenson

3. *Be flexible.* This doesn't really conflict with a regular bedtime schedule. Routines are convenient, but need not be rigid. There can be good reasons for staying up late for a special occasion such as a party, an educational TV show, a cuddling conversation, gazing at the stars on a balmy summer night. Special occasions are what memories are made of.

4. *Allow a toy.* Children have rituals, things they like to do with special blankets, toys, and cuddly friends. If something makes them happy, let them have it. If it's dirty, wash it; if it's raggedy, sew it. They'll love it just as much with patches.

5. *Respect a child's rhythm.* Most young children fit into normal bedtimes, but as children grow to high school and college age their biological time clocks may simply not match your ideas of sleeping and waking. Ensure that children get *enough* sleep to maintain good health, but don't be quite so uptight about whether a teen-ager goes to bed at 10 or stays up reading until midnight.

6. *If a child is really frightened at night, comfort him.* A child who gets out of bed every night simply because he doesn't want to miss something is one thing; but if he is truly frightened, that's another matter. Those sinister shadows moving on the wall and those noises creeping in can be terrifying to a four-year-old. Five minutes for a soothing back rub and an impromptu I-love-you song can make a big difference in a child's feelings toward his bed and the world in general.

Talk about dreams and nightmares with a child so he learns that everyone has them and he is not experiencing some frightening horror all alone. If a child prefers a small light, or a radio on, or the door open, permit him to have it. You can always turn off the radio after he's asleep.

The Night Terror

All the pieces are not yet in place, nor are their relationships clear, but as of now it appears that the Stage IV nightmare is not merely a more intense bad dream but a psychic experience of another kind entirely. Indeed, a picture of man's interior being is emerging which suggests that each of us lives not one but three separate mental lives: the life of the waking daytime mind, the life of the normal dreaming mind and the life of the mind in deep sleep, when the night can suddenly be filled with inner terror.

Edwin Diamond

SLEEP HARDWARE

The bed plays a central role in human life. It is the place where people are born, where they go for solace, sickness, and sex. It is where they spend a third of their lives in sleep; it is usually where they die.

Physically, the bed is important for keeping the body sheltered and warm, and for freeing it of its full weight, making rest possible. Psychologically, it is much more: a haven, a retreat, a place of escape, security and respite for renewing and restoring mind and body.

Today, sleepers and nonsleepers support a multi-million dollar industry catering to sleep needs. Americans spend $1 billion a year on mattresses alone.

In addition, people spend money on sleeping pills, water beds, bead beds, vibrator beds, eye shades, ear plugs, stereo records, fancy lights, and an incredible array of mechanical devices which include air purifiers, vibrators, head clamps and machines that emit soothing "white noise." There are LP record albums sold by Hammacher-Schlemmer in New York City that do nothing but hum to soothe the restless sleeper. Other records play sounds of waterfalls or the surf.

Norman Dine, curator of an insomniac haven in East Orange, New Jersey, called the "Sleep Center," provides his clients with, for example, tape-recorded exhortations from a minister or psychiatrist such as "You hate to face reality because you think you don't

Sleep and Atmospheric Pressure

Barometric pressure also affects sleep. When routine check-ups, including EEGs, were done on airline crews, it was found that the days the men fell asleep while the test was being done were the days that the atmospheric pressure was low.

A sleep fact

measure up." He also sells an ejecting bed which, at the proper hour, catapults a sleeper out of bed.

Dine's catalog also lists a "womb bed" inside a curtained lucite cell; a king-size foam latex slide-apart canopy bed; a twin "culture bed" containing book shelves, record player and plastic top for eating; or a double bed with one hard side, one soft. Pillows come in all shapes and sizes, some with cutouts, others specially contoured, one with a speaker that lets a night-owl listen to the radio while his or her bedmate sleeps.

Dealers say people now are buying longer and wider beds, harder mattresses and fluffier pillows than ever before. Hein and Kapins, Inc., a New York firm, makes custom beds for sleepers who want plenty of room. They also feature vibrating beds that rock you to sleep with a gentle motion; electrical beds that go up, down, and even around; and the "Aquarest" bed, a bathtub-like device full of circulating salt water in which the body floats.

Some devices are quite ingenious: a snore mask that's tied around the snorer's jaw; a "Slumber Tone" device that provides a steady, comforting sound which the manufacturer claims is similar to that of the prenatal environment; a "Robot Cigarette Holder" that lets a sleepy person smoke while his cigarette rests safely in the holder.

A French slumber shop in Paris called "Boutique du Sommeil" features a machine that shows colored patterns on a screen to calm the nerves. In France and in Japan you can buy electrosleep machines to use at home, and in the Soviet Union there are sleep stations where patients in beds are plugged to a communal electrical supply.

Animal Sleeping Habits

Some animals close their eyes when they sleep, some even cover their eyes with their paws or tail. And some animals with particularly sensitive ears, like the big-eared bat, sleep with their outer ears folded.

Other animals such as the antelope and some deer are thought not to close their eyes, in fact not to really sleep at all in our sense of the term, simply catching a few snatched moments at a time, but sleeping very deeply at those times.

A fish or snake cannot close its eyes since it has no eyelids. Frogs and salamanders do not sleep, but simply have periods of quiet.

Despite the commonly-held opinion, horses do lie down and sleep, sometimes for as much as seven hours at night.

Cows sleep with their eyes open and often go on chewing the cud. Dolphins apparently sleep for a couple of hours with one eye closed, then the other.

A sleep fact

REMEDIES FOR
INSOMNIACS

INSOMNIACS

At night, many people lie in bed, tossing and turning, staring into the darkness, punching their pillows, willing their minds to turn off. But sleep will not come.

The person who has trouble sleeping is not alone: an estimated 30 million people in the United States suffer from chronic insomnia. And probably most non-insomniacs have occasional periods when they wonder if they'll make it through a sleepless night.

In fact, doctors say that insomnia is one of the nation's most frequent medical complaints. And with today's daily tensions and stresses, nightly insomnia problems are becoming more widespread — alarmingly so, according to some physicians.

There are two major kinds of insomniacs: (1) people who can't fall asleep when they go to bed, and (2) people who fall asleep readily but can't *stay* asleep. Under age 50, difficulty in falling asleep is most frequent. Over age 50, the second type of insomnia — waking up frequently or early — is the primary problem.

Jacqueline Susann, an example of the inability-to-go-to-sleep type, spends many nights on the telephone

An American Insomnia Foundation

There is an implicit feeling that insomnia has a low priority among the ills that plague us. People do not seem to die of insomnia, and it would be hard to visualize an urgent, heart-rending television appeal for an American Insomnia Foundation. But it also would be hard to convince a chronic insomniac in his tossing and turning that his disorder is not serious.

Dr. Allan Rechtschaffen
Dr. Lawrence J. Monroe

with other insomniac friends. Insomniac Benjamin Franklin exemplified the middle-of-the-night awakening kind. He hypothesized that his problem was a rumpled bed; he solved it by buying a second bed, and whenever he awoke in the middle of the night he simply crawled from the bed he was in to the neatly made second bed to complete his night's sleep.

Dr. Dale C. Friend, of Harvard University Medical School, classifies insomnia according to its four causes:

1. *Tension insomnia,* recently described as "executive insomnia" by the *Journal of the American Medical Association,* is most common among bleary-eyed executives and other people who continually worry about their business. Tensions accumulated during the day still simmer inside at bedtime and can't (or won't) come out.

2. *Fatigue insomnia.* This includes people who get so tired during the day that they usually fall asleep after dinner. After a two-hour nap, they can't fall asleep at bedtime.

3. *Discomfort insomnia.* People who wake up during the night because of pain or discomfort from arthritis, ulcers, stomach upsets, toothache, and so forth, fall into this category.

4. *In-and-out insomnia* describes people who swear they "never slept a wink last night." In truth, they did, but they probably woke up frequently and remained on the borderline of light sleep stages all night, so that it seemed to them they had never really fallen asleep. Frequently elderly people complain that they just don't sleep like they used to anymore. Theirs is usually in-and-out insomnia.

An Ancient Writer's View

Dreams in general originate from those incidents which have most occupied the thoughts during the day.

Herodotus

Non-REM Dreaming

All people dream several times a night, the sleep researchers say; some just don't remember their dreams or may think that they are really awake with their thoughts. Usually these people, when awakened, do admit to dreams or images. One typical housewife still maintained after being awakened that she was not dreaming. "I was just playing with images . . . I was wide awake, really." But the EEG showed she was asleep and the researcher said she was snoring.

A sleep fact

In addition, everyone is plagued with what scientists call "situational insomnia" arising from temporary anxieties, a special crisis, or situations accompanied by tension and worry.

Dr. Allan Rechtschaffen, director of sleep research at the University of Chicago, found that insomniacs spend less time in REM sleep than normal sleepers. He says also that poor sleepers report a significantly greater number of psychosomatic and emotional problems, and on the whole are more psychologically disturbed than good sleepers.

Another study revealed that insomniacs tend to overestimate the time it takes them to fall asleep. When 16 insomniacs were asked how long it took them to go to sleep, their replies averaged 59 minutes, but according to the laboratory clock they required only 15 minutes on the average to fall alseep. A comparison group of 16 good sleepers took an average of 7 minutes to drop off.

The insomniac problem may be more one of changing the quality of sleep than increasing its duration, Rechtschaffen says. The good sleepers spent 92 per cent of the bed period asleep, as compared to 82 per cent for poor sleepers; so the two groups did not differ very much in *amount* of sleep. What did differ was the sleep quality.

Poor sleepers tend to have higher heart rates and higher body temperatures, and make more body movements throughout sleep. "Poor sleepers also tend to feel awake *during* sleep," reports Dr. Rechtschaffen, "which may account for the apparent exaggeration of reports of insomnia." Accordingly, treatment of insomnia should involve sleep quality as well as sleep quantity.

To Sleep

A flock of sheep that leisurely pass by,
One after one; the sound of rain, and bees
Murmuring; the fall of rivers, winds and
  seas,
Smooth fields, white sheets of water,
  and pure sky;
I have thought of all by turns and yet do
  lie
Sleepless! . . .
Come, blessed barrier between day and
  day,
Dear mother of fresh thoughts and
  joyous health!

William Wordsworth

Insomnia in Alarming Proportions

With our so-called urban civilization — with people less active than they used to be and with more tensions, more interruptions, more deadlines pressing in on them, flying back and forth across the country in a few hours — with all these changes, insomnia is reaching alarming proportions.

Dr. Anthony Kales

101

INSOMNIA SYMPTOMS

An insomniac should first determine what type of insomnia he experiences, and discover, if possible, what causes his particular problem, asking himself specifically why he cannot sleep.

For example, some people have a disturbance or pain that wakes them up. Certain medical problems might produce a sleep disturbance.

Some take long naps in the afternoon or evening which keep them from sleeping at night. Others are worried about something. Their job. Marriage. Children. Money. An impending crisis.

Try to eliminate the suspected cause of insomnia or put it out of mind. The exercises in Part II of this book may be helpful in overcoming a problem of this kind.

Those who cannot analyze or overcome the problem themselves should see a physician. Insomnia can have medical causes, involving a physical disorder, or an emotional one. For example, disturbed sleep can sometimes be a sign of depression or schizophrenia. In fact, approaching recovery of a *depressed* patient is often measured by improvement in sleep. And some patients with insomnia due to an emotional disorder are treated with antidepressants and psychotherapy.

One sleep specialist says he becomes concerned about patients only when they manifest sleep problems on more than half the nights over a period of one or two weeks.

Before final diagnosis of a sleep problem, another doctor has his patients keep a diary for one month, noting length and quality of sleep, major events of each day, and general feelings at night and in the morning.

Dreams Can Be Deceiving

**Divinations and omens and dreams
are folly,
and like a woman in travail
the mind has fancies.
Unless they are sent from the Most High
as a visitation,
do not give your mind to them.
For dreams have deceived many,
and those who put their hope in them
have failed.
Without such deceptions
the law will be fulfilled,
and wisdom is made perfect
in truthful lips.**

Ecclesiasticus 34:5–8

A third sleep expert reminds people that a short night's sleep is not necessarily insomnia. There are many people who don't *need* a lot of sleep. Don't worry about how much sleep you are "supposed" to have, he says, only about whether you get enough sleep to keep from being tired.

REMEDIES

In ancient Greece, Egypt, Babylon and China miraculous sleep remedies were offered in religious temples. Today, people hoping for sleep cures spend millions of dollars on tranquilizers and sleeping pills.

Recent studies show that one out of every two people has taken sedatives or tranquilizers at some time, and one in five uses them frequently.

Presently, more than 200 types of sleeping potions are available. During one year in the United States 800,000 pounds of barbiturates are sold — enough to supply some 50 doses to every man, woman and child in the country! Doctors prescribe tranquilizers more frequently than *any* other drug.

The problem is just as serious in other countries. A survey in Scotland shows that 15 per cent of men and 25 per cent of women over age 45 regularly take sleeping pills, and in Great Britain sleeping pills — 10 per cent of all prescriptions — now outsell aspirin.

On and On

We are no longer a society that can cease productivity at sunset and arise at dawn to begin again.

Wilse B. Webb

A Mickey Finn

Chloral hydrate, the first modern sleeping remedy, was discovered about 80 years ago, and is now known chiefly as the main ingredient of the Mickey Finn.

A sleep fact

Pills are not always necessary. People can enjoy good natural sleep without them. Here are 22 ways without benefit of pills — advice from sleep experts throughout the world — for getting a good night's sleep even for those who usually have trouble sleeping:

1. *Exercise more.* Increased activity makes going to sleep easier and increases total sleep time as well as Stage 4 sleep. However, don't exercise just before bed as it tends to mobilize muscles and stimulate physical activity.

2. *Don't go to bed until sleepy.* Lying in bed wide awake tends to frustrate a would-be sleeper. Remain up till tiredness begins to overtake the body.

3. *Go to bed at the same time every night.* Try to establish by experimentation the best time for you to sleep, then faithfully follow that schedule except for special occasions. But, remember rule 2, and don't go to bed at the usual hour unless you feel sleepy and drowsy.

4. *Have a snack.* Some people feel better when they eat or drink something before going to bed. Milk seems to soothe most people. If eating disturbs sleep, stay away from food.

5. *Live by personal natural rhythms.* The sleepy person should go to sleep. The wide-awake person should stay up. The internal clock is a better indicator of sleep needs than the clock on the wall.

Bears Don't Really Hibernate

Surprisingly, bears, which most of us think of as hibernators, do not really hibernate. They fatten up tremendously and crawl into a hole and sleep deeply. Periodically through the winter, they wake up and may even go out and look around a bit. Female bears give birth in midwinter, and then stay warm and awake from time to time to tend the cubs. Hibernation is apparently controlled by biological time clocks just as our sleep cycles are, but with rhythms based on longer seasonal cycles and long cyclic changes in hormones rather than on a 24-hour rhythm.

A sleep fact

6. *Establish a routine.* Use whatever behavior pattern helps, no matter how stupid it might seem. Some have warm milk and cookies, others brush their hair exactly 53 times, some stand on their heads, or hug a teddy bear goodnight, or punch a pillow three times. Dickens always slept with his head pointing north! Experiment: try a warm bath; pillow, no pillow; freezing cold, warm; window open, window shut.

7. *Don't take long naps in the afternoon or naps in the evening.* Avoiding naps helps make insomniacs more tired at night and more ready for sleep.

8. *Sleep less.* Some people really don't have insomnia. If after a night of less than usual sleep a person feels good and is not dragging around tired, maybe he doesn't really require as much sleep as he thought he did. Maybe he is one of the blessed people who can get by on less!

9. *When sleep doesn't come, get up.* Don't just lie there, do something. Read. Study. Write letters. Clean out closets or files. Compile a Christmas list. Sort recipes. Mentally redecorate the room. Balance the checkbook. Start a self-education program in some interesting subject.

10. *If a problem arises in the mind, think about it.* Don't let the mind clutch and whirl around a dozen current problems. But pick one and think it through, find out what's behind it, what can be done about it.

Sleep and Acupuncture

According to acupuncturists, there are three crucial points that affect sleep: two on the heel and one above the elbow. Inserting the needles at these points will treat insomnia, they say. Since it is still difficult to obtain acupuncture treatment outside of China, some do-it-yourselfers claim they gain benefits by scratching these areas with a fingernail, or holding a hot object about a quarter of an inch from the skin.

A sleep fact

Monotonous Sounds Promote Sleep

Why is it that some types of monotonous sound promote sleep while others prevent it? Perhaps the sound of a dripping faucet interferes with sleep because of a component of annoyance directed either against ourselves or someone else, for not having turned off that faucet properly. Consciously, we may not even register the origin of our emotional disturbance; nevertheless, it ferments in us with increasing force and thus prevents us from relaxing and going to sleep.

Margaret Steger

11. *Use sleepless time to do mind-consciousness exercises* suggested in Part II. Lewis Carroll of *Alice in Wonderland* fame was, in public life, Professor Charles Dodgson, a lecturer in mathematics at Oxford University. He used to calm his insomniac mind by thinking of mathematical puzzles.

12. *Avoid stimulants.* Coffee, tea, cola, cigarettes can all keep people awake. Stay away from them, especially during after-dinner hours.

13. *Count sheep.* It really works, according to Dr. Richard Wyatt of the National Institute of Mental Health. "It's not so much the thinking about sheep," says Dr. Wyatt, "but doing a very repetitive and boring task. You know its outcome so you can't get anxious or excited." He says that psychological sleep difficulties in most cases stem from an active mind ruminating about some problem, and counting sheep can be a useful way of slowing down mental processes and falling asleep.

14. *Have a glass of wine, beer, or other beverage.* One or two drinks will often relax people so they can slip easily into a good night's sleep. Don't drink heavily, however, because an alcohol-sodden sleep cuts REM experience short and is not restful.

15. *Take two aspirins and go to bed.* Strangely enough, taking aspirin will often promote sleep, and sleep experts frequently recommend it.

16. *Think of pleasant, peaceful things.* Program the mind for relaxation. Push worries away and think of something pleasant that happened during the day, or if necessary during a past day.

17. *Keep a sense of humor.* Miserable as insomniacs feel, they admit sleeplessness is pretty silly. A little laughing just might bring on enough relaxation to fall asleep.

18. *Use progressive relaxation exercises.* Step-by-step outlines of these are presented in Part II.

19. *Try yoga.* Many of the yoga exercises provide enough tranquility and repose to relax.

20. *Practice breathing exercises.* Deep breathing also helps relaxation. Some are suggested in Part II.

21. *If none of these suggestions help, consider getting help from a psychologist or psychiatrist.* Or consult a sleep laboratory if there is one in your area. Experts there may be able to help you find the cause of your insomnia.

22. *Don't lose sleep over it.* Does it really matter how many hours tonight's sleep provides? Sleep missed tonight can always be recouped tomorrow night. Relax. Worrying makes it more difficult to let go. Remember, some people only *need* five hours of sleep a night.

Effective Sleep Learning

Researchers indicate that sleep learning is most effective during light sleep, and better toward morning. Sleep learning ability, they found, seems to improve with practice, but results are far from startling. Their conclusion: people will continue to do most of their learning while awake.

A sleep fact

ELECTROSLEEP FOR INSOMNIACS

Electrosleep is simple. A subject goes to the lab at any convenient time, stretches out on a bed for an hour, and receives mild electrical stimulation through electrodes on eyelids and head. All the person feels is a slight tingling sensation coming from the gentle, pulsed current which courses through the lower portions ot the brain for approximately 15 minutes.

Electrosleep has been reported to cure insomnia. For years, doctors in Russia have used it to treat insomnia and other medical problems. Soviet scientists pioneered electrosleep in the 1950s and, according to reports, successfully treated some 500,000 persons for varying problems including insomnia, stuttering, ulcers and hypertension.

Some American sleep researchers suspect that electrosleep works only by "placebo effect," that is, the treatment is effective not of itself, but only because the patient believes that it is helping him. Thus, certain patients who believe electrosleep treatment to be effective have fallen asleep, even when the electrosleep machine wasn't turned on.

People describing electrosleep therapy say that when the current is turned on it produces fellings of well-being and relaxation. Although therapy is usually given in the afternoon, its effects are still noted at bedtime.

Dr. Rosalind Cartwright, director of the University of Illinois Sleep Laboratory, reported the comments of volunteer electrosleep testers. One subject, an insomniac for years, said, "I don't know what they're doing to me, but I'm sleeping better than I have in years. I haven't felt so good since I was a kid. I feel like a new man."

At a recent meeting of the American Psychiatric Association, a Texas research team reported another series of experiments indicating electrosleep's value. Psychiatrists from the University of Texas tested

A New Therapy

Dr. Saul Rosenthal of the University of Texas at San Antonio has a middle-aged patient who has been a chronic insomniac since his teens. At various times the patient tried psychotherapy, hypnosis, and a long list of drugs. When he came in for electrosleep treatment in 1971, he was taking heavy nightly doses of both a tranquilizer and a sedative. After only five electrosleep sessions the patient was able to get to sleep every night thereafter without taking any sedative at all, although he continued to require a single tranquilizer on some nights.

Richard Deming

110

electrosleep therapy on twenty-two patients in five sessions, each lasting half an hour. Some received the therapy; some did not. By rating the patients' levels of anxiety and depression, and their sleep disturbance before and after treatment, the researchers concluded that the mental state of 8 out of 11 receiving therapy improved.

At the National Institute of Mental Health's Clinical Psychobiology Laboratory in Bethesda, Maryland, Drs. Frederick Snyder and Bernard Frankel caution patients not to expect magical improvements from electrotherapy. Some patients seem to benefit from the therapy while others do not.

Other doctors, working with "biofeedback," train people to relax their muscles so they can sleep easier. Persons are trained to develop control of the autonomic nervous system to affect certain body mechanisms usually not under voluntary control. Biofeedback has been used to treat high blood pressure, asthma, and insomnia. Subjects watch their brain wave rhythms on a monitoring machine and learn to control them.

The House of Inner Composure

I am entering a solemn house. It is called "the house of inner composure or self collection." In the background are many burning candles arranged so as to form four pyramid-like points. An old man stands at the door of the house. People enter, they do not talk and often stand still in order to concentrate. The old man at the door tells me about the visitors to the house and says: "When they leave they are pure." I enter the house now, and I am able to concentrate completely.

C. G. Jung
A patient's dream

111

IF SLEEPING PILLS ARE NECESSARY

Although natural sleep is best, there are times — for example, periods of grief or pain, or after surgery — when pills to aid sleep may be necessary. Age-old sleep remedies included hops, henbane, mandrake root, valerian and wormwood. Now druggists sell more sophisticated products such as chloral hydrate, barbiturates, antidepressants, Valium, Dalmone. But chemical sleep inducers produce cheap sleep — poor quality sleep and decreased REM — and usually leave sleepers with a hangover of sluggishness.

In even moderate doses, sleeping pills can produce side effects such as delayed reaction times, confusion, and skin rashes. In pregnant women, sleeping pills can cause deformities of the unborn fetus. Thalidomide, a once widely used sleeping pill, was not unique in producing negative effects on unborn infants.

Patients can also develop a tolerance to sleep-inducing drugs so that larger and larger doses are needed to produce sleep, sometimes reaching lethal levels. Sometimes body reactions to such drugs can vary so that a regular sleeping pill user can accidently take a lethal overdose.

But the commonest danger from sleeping pills is addiction. Some experts consider barbiturate addiction more difficult to cure than hard narcotic addiction. Such addiction may develop quickly even when the pills are taken for just a short time.

The Seasons of Sleep

They say that dreams are more sure and clear when they happen towards the end of the night, because then the vigor of the soul emerges, and heavy sleep departs. As to the seasons of the year, dreams are calmer in spring, since summer relaxes, and winter somehow hardens, the soul; while autumn, which in other respects is trying to health, is apt to enervate the soul by the lusciousness of its fruits . . . But however this be, I take it that it all amounts to ingenious conjecture rather than certain proof (although the author of the conjecture be no less a man than Plato) and possibly all may be no other than the result of chance.

Tertullian

Persons who feel they have to take pills should consult their doctor about the best ones for them. Take them as infrequently as possible, give them up as quickly as possible, and while taking them follow directions exactly.

Here is a summary of the various drugs often used as sleeping pills:

Barbiturates, the most common sleeping pills, can be valuable when used under proper medical supervision. In normal doses they depress action of nerves and skeletal muscles, slow down heart rate and breathing, and lower blood pressure. They also decrease amount of Stage 1 and REM sleep. Abuse or overdose can cause physical addiction, confusion, staggering, convulsions and even death.

Tranquilizers, widely used as relaxing drugs, were designed to help relieve anxiety. Relatively safe when taken in small doses, they can also be addictive and otherwise dangerous when misused. Excess tranquilizer dosages can cause confusion, impaired judgment, drowsiness, irritability and motor disturbance.

Antihistamines, mainly used for relief of allergies and cold symptoms, usually produce drowsiness as a side effect.

Other Drugs available over the counter as sleep products are compounds containing scopolamine and bromides. They can be toxic and may be dangerous to persons with certain medical conditions.

KICKING THE SLEEPING PILL HABIT

Giving up sleeping pills may produce withdrawal symptoms; these may include cramps, nausea, headache, delirium, convulsions and even death. People withdrawing from a sleeping pill habit often have terrible nightmares or may find they keep waking up at night.

Get off the pills gradually, working with a doctor. If withdrawal is difficult, it's sometimes necessary to spend a week or so in a hospital with proper supervision. There the drug addicted sleeper benefits from emotional support in the form of psychotherapy or counseling. When a patient stops using pills, it may take several months for his sleep to return to its normal pattern.

What happens to patients when they've been taking drugs in large doses for sleep over a long period and the drugs are withdrawn?

In general, if the drugs are withdrawn abruptly, people suffer from insomnia the first night or two. If they have been taking drugs that were also REM suppressants, when they do fall asleep they experience large REM overloads and very disturbed sleep, frequently awakening with nightmares or feelings of fear or oppression. But it is important not to go back on the drug and suppress REM sleep and dreaming again. This just perpetuates the problem.

The effect of a drug on a person's REM depends on a number of factors. First, is the drug long — or short-acting? If the drug is long-acting, more REM suppression builds up. Second, is the drug taken each night? If it is, more REM suppression occurs. Third, how long does the person sleep? If he's a short sleeper — four to six hours — the drug is active throughout his entire sleep period and so

Effects of Drugs on REM Sleep

Generally most drugs which significantly decrease REM sleep upon withdrawal are associated with a "rebound" compensatory increase in REM sleep often associated with nightmares.
The following is a brief list of drugs affecting REM sleep:
(a) Those Agents Causing a Reduction in REM Sleep.
Alcohol
Amphetamines
Barbiturates
Diphenythydantoin
Glutethimide
Imipramine and derivates
MAO inhibitors
Meprobamate
Morphine
(b) Those Agents Causing an Increase in REM sleep
Reserpine
Phenothiazines
(c) Those Agents Exhibiting Minimal or no Significant Effect on REM sleep.
Chloral Hydrate
Flurazepam
Methaqualone
Chlordiazepoxide

Gerald P. Sherman

suppresses REM sleep almost completely. If he is a long sleeper — eight to nine hours — and is using a short-acting drug, REM suppression weakens as the drug wears off.

The following table lists certain sleep-inducing drugs (some that produce dependency and some that do not) and their effect on REM sleep suppression and rebound.

Reported effect of drugs on the percentage of REM sleep.

	REM Suppression with Administration	REM Rebound following Withdrawal
Drugs that may produce dependency:		
Amphetamine	Yes	Yes
Phenmetrazine	Yes	Yes
Diethylpropion	Yes	Yes
Methylphenidate	Yes	?
Tranylcypromine	Yes	Yes
Barbiturate	Yes	Yes
Alcohol	Yes	Yes
Morphine	Yes	Yes
LSD	No	Yes
Glutethimide	Yes	Yes
Methyprylon	Yes	Yes
Meprobamate	Yes	Yes
Nitrazepam	Yes	Yes
Drugs that do not lead to dependency:		
Amitriptyline	Yes	Small or nil
Nialamide	Yes	Nil
Diphenylhydantoin	Yes	Nil
Chlorpromazine	Dose dependent	? Nil
Fenfluramine	Nil	Nil

Sleep Drug Abuse

The use of sleep drugs must be a major issue in any discussion of drug abuse in this country today.

Dr. Julius Segal

From Dr. Ian Oswald in *SLEEP: Physiology & Pathology*.

To minimize withdrawal symptoms, a drug should be withdrawn gradually. If a patient is taking 500 mg. of Nembutal, for example, he might decrease his dosage by 100 mg. every five to six days to minimize REM rebound and insomnia.

During any withdrawal, patients should expect an increase in dreaming and may even have disturbing dreams. This does not mean a change in personality or a disintegrating psyche; it is a purely temporary phenomenon.

Adverse Effects

All sleeping pills affect persons adversely for a minimum of 18 hours.

Dr. Malcolm H. Lader

119

ALCOHOL AND SLEEP

Although alcohol is not a sleeping pill, it is classified as a drug and is used by many to induce sleep.

Naturally, the question arises, *How does alcohol affect sleep?*

While many people find alcohol at bedtime helpful for relaxation, it also suppresses REM sleep. When 6 ounces of 95 per cent ethyl alcohol were given to normal subjects, REM was significantly reduced. Studies of "social" drinkers revealed no striking abnormalities in sleep patterns, but study of chronic alcoholics showed striking changes. Upon withdrawal, alcoholics experienced delirium tremens and spent almost 100 per cent of sleep time in REM. They apparently built up considerable REM debt from continual REM-deprivation, and it is believed that during withdrawal the resurgence of REM activity carries over into the waking state in the form of delirium tremens hallucinations.

Evidence is quite strong that alcohol in moderate-to-large amounts causes major interference with the REM mechanism, and in many ways approximates barbiturate usage. Barbiturate-like effects may not be noticeable in people who take three or four drinks every day as "social drinkers," but these effects may become obvious when they stop drinking. Heavy social drinkers often awaken in the morning feeling tremulous and take a drink to "calm" down.

Should alcohol be used to encourage sleep, then?

Doctors say that it depends on the amount. Certainly people who take large amounts of alcohol each night build up a tremendous REM deficit; they also experience very disturbed sleep.

Alcohol may, in small doses, help people to get to sleep, but it is a short-acting drug and therefore has little effect on sleep maintenance. Doctors report that alcohol helps their patients get to sleep, but then they waken and/or experience a REM rebound (overload) later on during the night. In either case disturbed sleep is the result.

In view of the negative effects of alcohol on sleep patterns, sleep experts, in general, do not recommend alcohol to alleviate sleep problems.

Comfort Causes Tension

The basic human activities of *lying*, *sitting, standing and walking*, which in a culture more attuned to the significance of these activities were called "the four dignities of man," offer the easiest opportunity of discovering our attitudes to our environment and the extent to which we are conscious of what we are doing. It is obvious that many people stand as little as possible because it tires them, sleep on mattresses that are carefully designed with much give to them and "sit" in overstuffed or contoured chairs, thereby to a great extent avoiding full contact with the environment. Rather than accept an environment which requires vitality and giving on their part, they seek one which permits them to maintain their "tensions" and flaccidities intact while actually supposing that this "easy life" brings "relaxation." Of course, the insulation from contact which all this "comfort" represents leads, like any insulation, to a degree of starvation and merely encourages the tensions to grow and actual rest to become ever more elusive.

Charlotte Selver

121

NO-SLEEP THERAPY

"In a real dark night of the soul," observed F. Scott Fitzgerald, "it is always three o'clock in the morning." An appropriate description of insomnia combined with depression. Doctors say many people who complain of insomnia are actually suffering from depression. Such people may simply have a case of the blues or they may be experiencing overwhelming despair and futility, and a feeling that life has lost its meaning. Some depression sufferers often sleep more but enjoy it less, others may be sleeping almost not at all.

A doctor in Germany has come up with a novel insomnia treatment: no-sleep therapy. Instead of giving a sedative to produce drugged sleep, he prescribes a purposefully sleepless night. Dr. Walter Schulte, Director of the Neuropsychiatric Clinic at West Germany's Tübingen University, said he got the idea when he was told by one of his severely depressed patients that she was able to snap out of her listless state and put in a full, happy day of work after spending a night without any sleep. Dr. Schulte and two psychiatrists recruited patients with varying degrees of depression and kept them awake for an entire night. Doctors and attendants encouraged the patients to walk about and converse; no one was allowed to doze even for a minute.

All of the depressed patients benefited from the no-sleep night, with severely disturbed patients displaying the most striking improvement. In some cases after the experiment, the investigators reported overnight disappearance of such symptoms as loss of appetite, suicidal tendencies, and depressive delusions. The researchers theorize that depression involves a disturbance in the normal 24-hour sleeping-waking cycle, and that a night of sleeplessness helps readjust the rhythm.

However, no-sleep therapy is not universally beneficial. The doctors reported that nondepressed patients were not helped by being kept awake. They simply became exhausted.

Too Much Rest

Too much rest itself becomes a pain.

> Homer

The Whole Night

It does not become a man of counsel to sleep the whole night through.

> Homer

The Torture of Sleep Deprivation

One sort of treatment used for those accused of witchcraft was the "tortura insomniae". Of all things in brain disease, calm and regular sleep is most beneficial; yet, under this practise, these half-crazed creatures were prevented night after night and day after day, from sleeping or even resting. In this way temporary delusion became chronic insanity, mild cases became violent, torture and death ensued.

Andrew Dickson White

SEX AND SLEEP

Do people sleep better after sexual intercourse? Should doctors prescribe sex for insomniacs?

Making love has been used for centuries as a means to get to sleep. It is well known physiologically that most people experience physical relaxation after orgasm. In fact, a number of insomniacs living alone say they sometimes masturbate as a way to relax enough to fall asleep.

Dr. Ismet Karacan, and his colleagues at the University of Florida, decided to study the effect of sex on sleep scientifically. They asked a group of young adults to abstain from sex for seven to ten days while their sleep patterns were measured. The night after the end of the period they were asked to come to the sleep lab within a few hours after having had sexual intercourse.

That night most of the group reported enjoying more relaxed and restful sleep, Dr. Karacan said. However, in EEG sleep patterns no difference was seen between deprivation and sex nights. "This illustrates the point," said Karacan, "that the EEG does not necessarily provide a neurophysiological measure of subjective feelings regarding sleep." So there is an emotional dimension to sleep that the machines cannot measure.

Another doctor says that for sex to work as a satisfying relaxant people must enjoy the experience and get really involved. The relaxing effects are hindered where people view sexual intercourse as an imposition or a problem. Those thinking, "He's very heavy," or "There are cracks on the ceiling," are probably not getting involved enough in the pleasure.

Some doctors believe that a number of insomniacs may have problems in sexual adjustment. If a person is tense, and several kinds of insomniacs are, he may be as bothered about sex as he is about other things.

Sleeping pills may cause some sex problems found in insomniacs. A number of patients accustomed to multiple doses of hypnotic drugs, spontaneously relate that their sex life is more satisfying and that they enjoy more sexual desire after stopping their drug habit.

If exercise before sleep is disturbing, as the experts say, why doesn't the physical exertion of sexual activity also disturb sleep? The special unmeasurable, pleasurable ingredient in sexual activity may account for the difference.

As one doctor observed, "To say the least, sexual intercourse can be quite different from jogging around the block."

DEALING WITH OTHER SLEEP PROBLEMS

HYPERSOMNIA

Hypersomniacs are the opposites of insomniacs. They need an excessive amount of sleep. Left alone, they will stay in bed and sleep all day, often sleeping as much as 16 to 18 hours per day.

In some people the problem is chronic; in others it is rather rare, occurring only three or four times a year. The person will sleep for 18 to 20 hours a day for 3 or 4 days; then he feels fine and returns to his normal activities.

Sometimes hypersomnia is caused by various physical disorders: uremia, diabetes, brain concussion, encephalitis, or brain tumors. Other times the cause can be psychogenic — for example, when people sleep for long periods to escape some overwhelming anxiety.

Some hypersomniacs sleep all day. Others begin sleep at night but can't wake in the morning, often sleeping on until noon or later. Some hypersomniacs also experience what is called sleep drunkenness, a state of stumbling confusion that lasts for as long as two hours after awakening. Usually, excessive sleeping and sleep drunkenness runs in families. No one yet knows why.

Unfortunately, most physicians fail to check patients for symptoms of hypersomnia; the patient usually doesn't mention it since, often enough, his family attributes his hypersomnia to laziness or an unusual personality.

Research on hypersomnia is being done in several sleep centers. Drs. Bendrich Roth and Sonia Neosimalova of Prague, and Dr. Allan Rechtschaffen of the University of Chicago, describe the condition of hypersomnia with sleep drunkenness (HSD) this way:

Common Sleep Disorders

The two disorders of excessive sleep encountered most often by the clinical practitioner are probably narcolepsy and hypersomnia. Both are often mis-diagnosed and mistreated.

Drs. Allan Rechtschaffen
and William C. Dement

Sleeping Sickness

There is a disease called sleeping sickness. It is caused by a virus, sometimes occurs in epidemics, a severe one occurring just after World War I. The victims are overwhelmed by persistent sleepiness, and can die from the disease. The virus lodges in the brain stem where the central sleep pathways are.

A sleep fact

Light and Heavy Sleepers

Some animals are light sleepers and some heavy sleepers. Scientists believe this is due to the amount of danger they are in. Animals that are deep sleepers are either predatory with few enemies of their own, or they have very safe sleeping places. Animals that sleep fitfully or for very short periods are those subject to being preyed upon by their enemies at all hours.

This theory seems to prove out. Most hooved animals, such as sheep, goats and donkeys that graze for their food, go without much sleep. Predators, such as men and dogs, are good sleepers. Animals with safe dens, such as the fox, or mouse, sleep well. Antelopes, very vulnerable to attack, probably never sleep. Deer only sleep a few minutes at a time.

A sleep fact

"HSD patients rarely waken spontaneously at an appropriate time; they have to be awakened. They usually do not awaken to the ringing of a clock or telephone, or, if the ringing is prolonged, they shut it off and return to sleep. Many patients have special devices for waking them up such as repeating alarm clocks and resonators. In most cases, these devices are ineffective, and the patients have to be awakened by their family members. Awakening procedures must be vigorous and persistent; it is usually necessary to shake the patient repeatedly before he reacts. Even then the patients are confused, disoriented, very slow and unable to react adequately to external stimuli. If left alone, they often return to sleep and later do not remember having been previously awakened. In most cases, their state improves after washing with cold water but in many patients SD persists even then. Sometimes the movements of the patient are unco-ordinated, especially the gait, which is similar to the gait in alcoholic drunkenness."

Hypersomniac patients often report late to work and are, therefore, often considered undependable. Many are more or less drowsy all day and frequently fall asleep against their wills. "Falling asleep in the evening was reported as extremely rapid by the great majority of our patients," say the doctors. "Many claimed to fall asleep within seconds after going to bed; they are unable to read five lines before falling asleep."

Many patients stated they had suffered from HSD since childhood, and in many patients no other disease could be found which could be considered as a cause of the disturbance.

"A most surprising result," the doctors reported, "was that the heart and respiratory rates of the HSD patients were faster than those of all other groups. These results underscore the folly of automatically inferring lowered metabolism in cases of excessive sleep — a mistake which is often made in the diagnosis of hypersomnia."

Many people with hypersomnia never seek medical help for the disorder. Treatment for hypersomnia usually involves taking stimulant drugs at bedtime, or if an evening pill disturbs sleep, someone makes them take the drug upon awaking in the morning.

NARCOLEPSY

In narcolepsy, people fall asleep irresistibly during the day for periods of about ten to fifteen minutes, then wake up feeling fine.

People may fall asleep at a desk, in a restaurant, or in the middle of talking or making love. Narcolepsy attacks are especially likely to occur after meals. They apparently are caused by physical factors, not psychological ones, and have nothing to do with metabolic rates or the thyroid, as is sometimes thought.

The American Medical Association estimates that 400,000 to 600,000 people in the United States suffer from narcolepsy. The disorder is basically an "attack" of uncontrollable sleep, but may also include a sudden attack of paralysis. The accompanying paralysis may be precipitated by something as simple as a loud noise or laughing.

A major problem with narcolepsy, according to researchers Drs. Allan Rechtschaffen and William C. Dement, is that patients, without realizing they have a physical illness, build up terrible guilt feelings and embarrassment, and are not aware that medicines exist that can help them.

Patients are tremendously relieved to learn that narcolepsy involves normal sleep and that these sleep attacks are not symptomatic of psychotic or epileptic conditions, the doctors say. "One of our patients, a very eager and responsible college teacher, was amazed to learn that she had a specific sleep disorder and that she was not pathologically lazy as she had believed. For over forty years, she had had to live with an unnecessarily distorted self-concept."

In addition, the doctors state that employers, failing to understand that the narcoleptic suffers from uncontrollable sleep, often fire what they consider to be lazy or irresponsible workers who might be able to perform very adequately if they are granted one or two short naps a day.

To Sleep Again

I go to bed at midnight but it is understood that I shall go on sleeping until midday, that is, for twelve hours instead of the seven or at most eight that I used to sleep before this period of my life. I sleep for twelve hours instead of seven not because I am tired or in any way ill, but because I succeed, by this means, in obliterating twelve hours out of the twenty-four that I am compelled to live through each day. After about seven hours of sleep, I wake up regularly; this is the moment when formerly I used to rise and dress and start living. But I have only to think of the life I should be living if I got up, in order to desire immediately to escape from it. And so instead of getting out of bed . . . I take a pill, then take another, turn out the light, nestle down again, pulling the covers over my head and very soon I fall asleep again.

Alberto Moravia

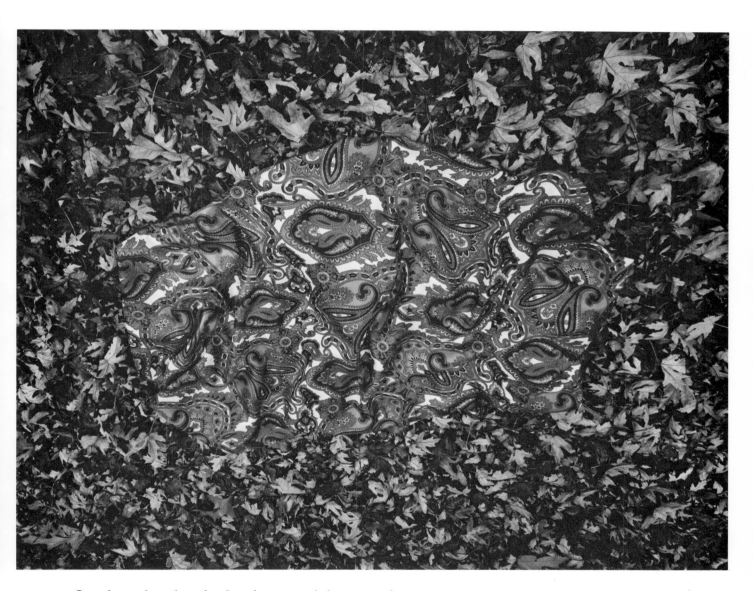

On the other hand, the doctors claim, certain nar-
coleptics should not be allowed to drive. About 10
per cent of narcolepsy patients admit to one or more
automobile accidents as a result of dozing off while
driving. Medical treatment is similar to that for
hypersomnia — amphetamines several times daily, or
sometimes Ritalin.

After a Nightmare

Had it been simply waking, he would have been obliged to them for the noise that disturbed him; for, in that case, he would have been relieved from the tortures of hell-fire, to which, in his dream, he fancied himself exposed. But this dreadful vision had been the result of that impression, which was made upon his brain by the intolerable anguish of his joints; so that, when he awaked, the pain instead of being allayed, was rather aggravated by a great acuteness of sensation.

Tobia Smollett

NIGHTMARES

People sometimes dream of horrifying, terrifying, fearful things. Monsters chasing them. Situations of mortal danger. They may try to scream and not be able to. They may feel paralyzed, unable to move or to fight off the smothering, ominous thing. Finally, they awaken in a cold sweat, their hearts beating wildly. These are nightmares, generating fear and panic in the night.

Night terror, another kind of sleep problem, may be described as a rare, extremely terrifying form of nightmare. According to Dr. Charles Fisher of Mt. Sinai Medical Center in New York, during a night terror sleepers heart rates may skyrocket in a few seconds to 160 or 170 beats per minute — "a rate of acceleration greater than in any other human response, including severe exercise or orgasm." Fisher says persons in the grips of a night terror may also gasp, moan, groan, curse, or let out blood-curdling, piercing screams, or sleepwalk in a panic.

Children who experience night terrors may scream out in the middle of the night, sobbing and crying for their mother. Sometimes even while clutching at her, they are still asleep and unaware that she is present. Between the ordinary nightmare and the panic of a night terror, there is more than just a difference in severity. Three distinctions are clear:

First, according to Dr. Fisher, the nightmare is an anxious dream in the REM stage; the night terror usually occurs in delta sleep during Stages 3 and 4 early in the night.

Second, REM nightmares deal with controlled anxiety; they are actually prolonged dreams, lasting around 20 minutes. In contrast, a night terror is un-controlled anxiety, a panic so severe it sometimes propels the victim out of bed, sends him racing through the house in fright. It is not an ongoing dream, but a "sudden, instantaneous cataclysmic event," states Fisher. It happens during very deep sleep; the deeper the sleep, the more severe may be the fear and terror. A night terror can sometimes be set off by awakening a person from the deep stages of sleep.

Third, REM dream nightmares are fairly common. Night terrors, however, are believed to occur in only about 4 per cent of school children, less often in adults. However, some people experience them steadily from childhood through their entire lives, sometimes even several times in one night. In adults, night terrors — often a consequence of severe trauma-tic experiences — usually involve visions of suffoca-tion, entrapment, heavy weights upon the chest.

Severe nightmare problems or night terrors can be helped by several medicines, if they cannot be over-come by nondrug means. One effective medicine cited by physicians is Diazepam, a tranquilizer.

A Psychotic Episode

Other researchers have come to regard the true nightmare not so much as a dream but as an encapsulated psychotic episode. Cambridge psychiatrist, John Mack, has noted the similarity between the night terror and one particular form of psychosis, the acute schizophrenic episode. Nightmares, he observes, may "progress" to an acute psychosis, co-exist with psychotic states or alternate with them. The fundamental difference between the two is the "instant re-versibility" of the nightmare — after a few moments the aroused nightmare victim is able to distinguish dream from reality. Once reassured he can quickly fall back to sleep.

Edwin Diamond

133

SLEEPWALKING

To walk in one's sleep is not uncommon; in fact, says the American Medical Association, some four million Americans have sought medical help for sleepwalking.

The condition is just as described of Lady Macbeth: "You see, her eyes are open." "Ay," replies the servant woman, "but their sense is shut."

There are reports of sleepwalkers driving cars, boarding planes, crossing from the rooftop of one tall building to another, setting the table for dinner, going swimming, and performing other complex actions.

Sleepwalkers act and move in the real world, but their consciousness remains in the realm of sleep. Upon awakening, they usually have no memory of the incident.

Scientists have learned some interesting things about sleepwalking. Psychiatrists Anthony Kales and Allan Jacobson of the University of California, Los Angeles, studied sleepwalkers and found they were not acting out dreams, as previously believed. In fact, subjects walked in their sleep only during the deep, slow-wave periods when there were no REMs.

They also found that sleepwalking in young children always began with a sudden burst of high-voltage brain-wave activity.

In general, sleepwalkers will not try to harm themselves. However, they tend not to notice dangers like cars bearing down on them and 20 foot drop-offs, so they frequently *do* get hurt, despite old wives' tales to the contrary.

Sleepwalkers should sleep on the first floor because they have been known to go out of windows. Also, when there is a known sleepwalker in the house, put away dangerous objects and car keys, and consider installing a special latch on the door.

Most children who sleepwalk outgrow the condition in two to three years. With adult sleepwalkers, psychotherapy is often indicated and sometimes certain drugs are recommended.

According to Doctors Kales and Jacobson, a child may start sleepwalking when parents are arguing a lot, when there is a death of a parent, the loss of a pet, distressing pressures at school, or a move to a new house.

Researchers have also found that certain pressures often cause sleepwalking in adults — for example, death of a loved one, or a new environment.

There may be a hereditary factor in sleepwalking also. Dr. Harry Bakewin of New York University reports that the chances of having a sleepwalking child are six times greater when one or both parents have sleepwalked. A doctor in Italy once reported an entire family of sleepwalkers: husband, wife, and four children. One night all six were sleepwalking at once!

Doctors agree that it is best not to awaken a sleepwalker abruptly but to leave him alone, unless he is potentially dangerous to himself or others. Usually if the sleepwalker is not interrupted, he will complete his mission and return to bed.

Watching a Sleepwalker

In a typical attack of somnambulism or sleepwalking the individual sits up quietly generally an hour or two after falling asleep, gets out of bed, and moves about in a confused and clumsy manner. Soon his behavior becomes more coordinated and complex. He may avoid objects, dust tables, go to the bathroom, or utter phrases which are usually incomprehensible. It is difficult to attract his attention. If left alone, he goes back to bed. A great deal of stimulation is required to awaken him. And when he is awakened he has little if any recollection of his sleepwalking activities and no recollection of dreaming.

Dr. Roger J. Broughton

If a sleepwalker must be awakened, never seize him and shake him awake, but call his name until it penetrates his consciousness. When he responds, help him realize where he is and reassure him that he is safe. Usually, someone can guide him gently back to bed without waking him.

Never punish a child for sleepwalking. Simply protect him from injury by putting gates at the heads of stairways and latching bedroom windows tightly.

If episodes last much more than about ten minutes, researchers suggest that a physician be contacted to make an examination for possible more complex causes of the sleepwalking experiences.

Laughing and Snoring

Laugh and the world laughs with you; snore and you sleep alone.

Anthony Burgess
Inside Mr. Enderby

Snore Noise Levels

Noise levels are measured in decibels. The lowest decibel count for snoring was forty, the same level as a quiet conversation. Some snores sent the decibel meter up to sixty-nine, close to the noise level of a jackhammer at ten feet.

A sleep fact

A World of Snorers

About one out of four adults snores occasionally and about half of these are regular snorers. More men than women snore, but there are many women snorers. Children seldom snore, except if they have enlarged tonsils or adenoids.

A sleep fact

SNORING

What can be more frustrating than lying awake, desperately tired, trying to shut out someone else's snoring? There are some 300 patented devices designed to decrease snoring — none of them guaranteed to work.

Snoring is caused by air going past the soft palate and uvula, that soft little piece of tissue hanging down in the back of the throat. When there is an obstruction in the breathing process, the air goes faster and causes the noise.

Here are some tips offered by doctors to reduce snoring:

Try increasing the humidity in the bedroom. Dry, swollen membranes can sometimes cause snoring.

Check for allergies. They can also cause swelling of tissue. One doctor reported a patient who stopped snoring after he eliminated tomatoes from his diet; another found a certain cheese was his problem.

Many hayfever sufferers snore, but usually only during ragweed season.

Avoid sniffing. One cause of snoring is collapse of nostril "flares." Collapse can be partly alleviated by massage, avoidance of sniffing, and by wearing little dilators at night to hold nostril flares open.

Sleep on your side. Most people snore more on their backs. Pile pillows behind the back to keep from turning over.

Try giving up smoking and drinking. This is often helpful, and worth a three-month trial.

Mouth devices sometimes help. Some sleepers benefit from chin straps that keep the mouth shut, or orthodontic appliances that keep the jaw from falling back.

Surgery. An operation seldom helps snoring unless some specific malady exists which can be corrected, such as a crooked or broken nose, enlarged tonsils or adenoids.

A Device to Stop Snoring

In 1950 Cyrus H. Johnston of Richmond, Missouri, received a patent on a device to prevent snoring. It was a metal yoke that strapped around the neck and prevented the mouth from opening during sleep, thereby forcing the sleeper to breathe through his nose . . .

It was the 275th issued for a device to stop snoring.

Richard Deming

Close Your Mouth

Q—May anything be done to correct or prevent sleeping with the mouth open?

Close it!

Q—How may this be done when asleep?

Make the suggestions to self when going to sleep. Get the system balanced, and this will be done.

Edgar Cayce

ASLEEP AT THE WHEEL

What causes sleepy-driver accidents? How many accidents are really caused by drivers falling asleep? What can be done to prevent them from happening?

In 21,000 highway accidents investigated in Oklahoma over 11 years, sleepy-drivers were estimated to account for 22 per cent.

In a study of California drivers involved in single-car accidents, the investigating officer cited 19 per cent as fatigued or asleep. The United States Bureau of Motor Carrier Safety reports that about 40 per cent of the fatal commercial crashes investigated involved a driver who was fatigued, inattentive, or asleep.

How do you discover a driver who is apt to fall asleep?

Dr. Robert E. Yoss of the Mayo Clinic devised an ingenious test to reveal narcolepsy and other degrees of sleepiness that are dangerous on the road. The subject sits in total darkness, staring at a target for ten minutes — a condition which simulates boring night driving. Meanwhile, an electronic apparatus measures pupil diameter and behavior as well as eyelid behavior.

Under test conditions, persons with narcolepsy became sleepy in minutes, sometimes sooner.

Many "normal" people also have trouble staying awake. One man who dropped to an unsafe level before the test was over was a commercial pilot for an airline! A psychiatrist who dropped to the same level piloted a private plane. In his office he often had trouble remaining awake while patients related their problems.

Dr. Yoss suggests his test become a standard part of state driver licensing procedures, so that sleep-prone people will be licensed only with restrictions noted on the license, in the same way vision restrictions are indicated.

For those who tend to get sleepy behind the wheel, here are some experts' suggestions:

1. People on long trips should avoid overextending themselves, get enough sleep, get an early start, take frequent rest stops.

2. Those who must drive for long hours at a stretch should be aware that driving performance necessarily deteriorates after three or four hours.

3. Drivers who miss a night's sleep and must travel should avoid alcohol or tranquilizers, but should eat. Lack of food can lower blood sugar and cause drowsiness.

4. If the vehicle has a radio, listen to a talk show or news program instead of music, which may be too soothing.

5. If possible, try playing games as long-distance truck drivers do, e.g., look for license plate number combinations, or count out-of-state cars. But avoid monotonous, sleep-inducing games such as counting telephone poles.

6. Drivers who know they tend to get sleepy behind the wheel should avoid driving at night, or after insufficient sleep.

7. Drivers who tend to get sleepy easily should see a physician. He may prescribe a stimulant to take before driving.

8. Passengers with a sleepy driver should talk to him, switch on the radio, suggest a rest break, or drive for a while. Be firm.

BED-WETTING

An estimated five million children in the United States suffer from the inconvenience and embarrassment of bed-wetting.

Bed-wetting — the medical word for it is enuresis (en-you-REE-sis) — is often difficult to understand, difficult to prevent, and difficult to correct. But it can be dealt with successfully with patience and proper professional medical help.

Generally, a boy at age four or four and a half can stay dry all night; a girl may get through the night successfully as much as a year sooner. By age five, about nine out of every ten children achieve bladder control both day and night. Many who continue to wet the bed at night will outgrow their bed-wetting soon thereafter, but in many others it persists for years, so it is important to give them help.

Enuresis can be caused by physical abnormalities in the urinary structures: weak bladder muscles, nerve damage or irritations, infection or pinworms. Or it can be a secondary symptom associated with diseases such as diabetes, epilepsy or sickle cell anemia. It may be associated with spicy foods or excessive fatigue. Or it may have psychological causes such as fear of the dark, too much work-a-day pressure, jealousy of a new baby, emotional instability, difficulty in school, harsh treatment from parents, or feelings of insecurity. Some children lose control because of frightening dreams; excitement or fear can have the same effect in an adult.

The causes of bed-wetting are difficult to ferret out. Treatment needs to be aimed at the specific cause, hence it is best to consult a family doctor or pediatrician for advice. He can do a thorough physical examination and carefully look into a child's medical history for possible causes.

If no structural defects or other physical causes are found, parents and physician can work together to explore possible psychological causes. For example, if bed-wetting is fairly recent and occurs after a child has already achieved night control, review recent events or mental conflicts that might be factors. Did something threaten him? Did he bring home a bad report from school? Is there a new baby in the family that made him regress to baby behavior to gain attention? Did he have to give up a room of his own

Outside My Control

I knew that bed-wetting was (a) wicked, and (b) outside my control. The second fact I was personally aware of, and the first I did not question. It was possible, therefore, to commit a sin without knowing you committed it, without wanting to commit it and without being able to avoid it.

George Orwell

to share it with someone? Are parents divorced, separated, or constantly bickering or using the child to vent their anger? Is he the dull one in a bright family, or do people compare him unfavorably in other ways with brothers or sisters? Has he just entered a new school or moved into a new neighborhood?

Several things can be done to help bed-wetters. Don't start bladder training too early. If you meet resistance in early attempts, wait until later. Never punish or shame a child younger than three for being physiologically incapable of control. Avoid excess intake of fluid in the late afternoon and early evening.

See that the child always empties his bladder before going to bed. Some parents find it helpful to awaken a child to urinate before they retire.

144

After a bed-wetting experience, help a child regain his sense of honor and his faith in himself. Encourage him to accept responsibility for his own bladder function. Have him talk to his pediatrician alone about learning to care for himself.

Try to diminish pressure on the child during the day, and try to ease any family stresses that may exist.

Let a bed-wetter older than eight or nine use an alarm clock. The child takes over responsibility for his bladder by setting his own clock, waking himself up and going to the bathroom. Most children will need to wake only once during a night, but a few twice.

When caused by too small a bladder, bed-wetting can often be cured by steadily increasing the bladder capacity. Most children double their bladder capacity between ages two and four. If the bladder does not enlarge naturally as it should, have the child force fluids during the day (just the reverse of what is usually practiced) and to hold the urine as long as possible to increase bladder capacity. A drug called Tofranil helps increase bladder capacity also.

Avoid excitement and excessive activity before bedtime. If too much nervous irritability persists, mild sedation may be indicated.

Avoid cocoa, spices, salt, and sweets, especially at dinner and most especially at night snacktime.

Talk the problem over with your child. Explain to him that he is old enough and capable enough to tell himself when to urinate. But don't rush him. Don't scold, nag, threaten, or suggest that there is anything shameful or dirty about wetting the bed. Give him self-assurance and love. Most important — relax.

Many physicians feel that the number of bed-wetters would decrease considerably if mothers would relax their toilet-training efforts. There are other, more important objectives than to have the youngest toilet-trained children in the neighborhood.

TOSSING AND TURNING

A healthy adult generally experiences from 20 to 60 body movements each night; these usually occur when he shifts from one sleep stage to another. Most aren't aware of turning and don't remember doing it, unless awakened immediately after movement. Physical activity in sleep may be increased in patients suffering from various clinical conditions.

Angina pectoris patients often complain of tossing and turning because they awaken frequently during the night and remain awake for considerable periods. Interestingly, these patients generally underestimate the number and duration of their body movements and awakenings. They suffer more than they report.

The Way It Is

I lie in bed.
I toss all night
in the cold unruffled deep
of my sheets and cannot sleep.

I see myself afloat
on the dead sea of my bed, falling away,
calling for help, but the vague scream
sticks in my throat.

Mark Strand

146

This inability to assess the amount of body movement or to report the number of awakenings is puzzling.

Strangely enough, the nose seems to be one of the things that makes people turn over at night. Dr. Maurice H. Cottle, an ear, nose and throat specialist at the University of Chicago Medical School, says the nose is actually a monitor of body rest and fatigue levels, and it causes you to shift body position during sleep to get the maximum relaxation for your body. When we breathe, the air passes alternately through the two sides of the nose, Dr. Cottle says. "It is a rhythmic alternating cyclic congestion and decongestion of the nose. This has been suggested as long as 100 years ago but has been reaffirmed with modern apparatus."

When people sleep on their left side, he explains, with the left nose buried in the pillow, the right nostril, right lung, and right side of the body contribute most to body function. When the right side becomes tired, the body shifts to a new position, putting the other side to work. The nose's cyclic activity is the trigger, and as the air supply is shut off on one side of the nose, the head turns to maintain an air supply. As the head turns, the body also shifts and turns. People who claim they remain immobile during the night and wake up in the same position as when they went to bed are simply not aware of their turning.

It is not just by accident that all these changes in body position occur. They are critical for survival during the sleep period. If a patient is unconscious and immobile for eight hours, he can develop complications as a result of not moving — pneumonia, skin ulcers, blood clots. Body movement is a mechanism that differentiates unconsciousness from sleep. In fact, in the management of an unconscious patient it is important to copy these sleep-related movements to prevent such complications.

Gross Body Movements

Sleep researchers report that gross body movements during REM sleep provide the demarcation point between separate episodes in a dream.

A sleep fact

Stress and Sleep

Stresses in the evening definitely carry over into sleep. Laboratory studies show that when people are subjected to horror films or other emotionally disturbing films before bedtime, they frequently carry the disturbing events into their sleep.

A sleep fact

Like a Distressed Ship

I was always tossing about like a distressed ship in a sea of bedclothes.

**Charles Dickens
David Copperfield**

WAKING UP

For a night-person, waking up can be a terrible ordeal. Sometimes it's not easy for a day-person either. It does little good to say that the early bird catches the worm.

But waking up can also be a pleasant experience, rather than a difficult one.

Here are eight basic rules for getting in gear in the morning:

1. *Don't get hung up on the problem of being a slow starter*. People who wake up dragging and slow may not have an emotional problem, but a physical one. In fact, there is a medical term for slow and difficult waking — dysania. People need not go around with guilt feelings or feelings of inferiority because they don't leap out of bed cheerful and smiling the way some others do.

2. *Know that many people suffer the same problem of dragging themselves out of bed*. Ben Franklin may have said, "Early to bed and early to rise makes a man healthy, wealthy and wise," but an equally venerable American — Robert Frost — used to milk his cows at midnight before he went to bed because he found it difficult to get up for milking early in the morning.

Pablo Picasso usually worked through the night and hated to get up in the morning. So did humorist Robert Benchley. Hungarian playwright, Ferenc Molnar was almost never awake until afternoon. Once when he was forced to get up early in the morning because of jury duty, he looked unbelievingly at the people crowding the Budapest streets and asked, "Are they *all* jurors?"

To See the Dawn

I understand why they execute condemned men at dawn. I just have to see the dawn in order to have my head roll all by itself.

Pablo Picasso

It Was A Cold Night

I dreamed that I was in a hotel, mounting many flights of stairs, until I entered a room where the chambermaid was making the bed; the white bedclothes were scattered over everything, and looked to me like snow; then I became conscious that I was very cold, and it appeared to me that I really was surrounded by snow, for the chambermaid remarked that I was very courageous to come up so high in the hotel, very few people venturing to do so on account of the great cold at this height. I awoke to find that it was a cold night, and that I was entangled in the sheets, and partly uncovered.

Havelock Ellis

Very Pleasant Like

I had a real horrorshow night's sleep, brothers, with no dreams at all, and the morning was very clear and like frosty, and there was the very pleasant like von of breakfast frying away down below. It took me some little time to remember where I was, as it always does . . .

A Clockwork Orange
Anthony Burgess

3. *Keep regular sleeping habits as much as possible.* A study of 600 persons in Florida showed that people who woke up best were those with regular sleeping habits. Adopt a fixed bedtime and arisal time and stick to it as much as is convenient.

4. *Try to get just enough sleep.* There is a great deal of variation in the amount of sleep that people seem to need. Each person has his own individual sleep needs. Once a person learns what his needs are, he should get that much: try not to get less, and also try not to get more. Unless people are catching up on lost sleep, getting too much sleep can have the same effect in the morning as not getting enough.

5. *Wake up one piece at a time.* Waking gradually can be a great help to the Great Trauma of Waking Up and Facing the Day. When still half asleep, instead of burrowing back into the pillow, bend one finger once, then twice. Make one small step toward waking up. Then bend each finger, slowly, calmly, then all ten. Now a toe, and another, then alternate your fingers and your toes, counting your wiggles as you go. After a few moments of this, the body has, without too much trauma, begun to get in tune with the world of the awake. Very few people can leap out of bed and jump into calisthenics, but doing fingerbends in bed isn't too much for anybody.

Next take a deep breath and hold it a while.

Then test the body. Move one arm, then the other. Bend one leg, then the other. Move the head. Stretch the whole body. Then really break the barrier. Sitting up, put both feet on the floor, move shoulders and arms around to the count of 4. Then stand up, arms high for 10 seconds. Then hang loose and limp for another 10 seconds. Do this stretch twice and be reasonably ready for the world.

People who find these exercises inappropriate or unappealing may invent some of their own; anything to ease themselves into the day without the usual fight.

The Roots of Nature

As human beings we have our roots in nature, not simply because of the fact that the chemistry of our bodies is of essentially the same elements as the air or dirt or grass. In a multitude of other ways we participate in nature — the rhythm of the change of seasons or of night and day, for example, is reflected in the rhythm of our bodies, of hunger and fulfillment, of sleep and wakefulness, of sexual desire and gratification, and in countless other ways.

Rollo May

6. *Try waking to music instead of an alarm clock.* In many primitive cultures, people refuse to wake another person because they believe that the soul wanders at night and may not have had enough time to get back into his body if awakened prematurely. In today's advanced culture, people jangle themselves awake with an alarm clock. Those who find alarms jarring to body and soul might try a clock radio and wake up gradually to soothing music.

7. *Think positively about the coming day.* Psychological attitudes toward waking up are probably most important: whether you *want* to get up or not, whether you are looking forward to the day or are wishing you could avoid it. It's helpful to prepare the mind at night by thinking of something pleasant to happen the next day.

Problems being avoided should be uncovered and faced. Then think of something pleasant or exciting to counteract the unpleasantness. If the something is unavoidable, try to deal with it so it is no longer bothersome.

If the problem can't be changed, arrange the morning schedule differently to allow time also for some special thing to make the day more pleasant — a walk in the early dawn, a half-hour for a hobby, a few minutes with a cup of coffee and conversation with the children before they go to school — whatever would help create good feelings about the day.

8. *Smile.* Somehow in our culture, waking up has acquired the reputation of being miserable. Others in the tribe groan and complain about waking up, and soon everybody's doing the same thing. People can learn to recondition themselves *out* of the morning grouch syndrome with a smile. Even if they don't mean it, it gets them into a better frame of mind.

Pretty soon they even learn to believe that waking up can be a beautiful beginning of another day.

A Bundle of Paradoxes

The bed is a bundle of paradoxes: we go to it with reluctance, yet we quit it with regret; we make up our minds every night to leave it early, but we make up our bodies every morning to keep it late.

Charles Colton

151

Practice

EXPLORING RHYTHMS

Sleep is an uncharted mystery that most people take for granted, without giving it much thought. Few of us begin to penetrate its meaning or its potential for our lives.

The following suggestions and exercises are designed to give a closer look at your own sleep world and the uncharted rhythms of your own body. Read the exercises, then try them. They're simple, fun, and will give you insight into your personal body rhythms.

1. TIME SENSE

PREPARATION

A sense of time is built into every living thing on earth. Humans still need to develop knowledge and control over their time-sense and sleep rhythms. Is personal time-sense some inner clock? Or does some outside force cause the rhythm? Scientists are still working to find answers. Probing rhythms. Probing sleep.

Plants and animals unconsciously keep track of time. How good is your conscious notion of time? The following exercise which can be done alone or with a friend will test this ability. It requires (1) a watch with a second-hand, and (2) a paper and pencil.

THE EXERCISE

Put a watch on a table so that its face is visible. When the second-hand reaches the top, at 12, look up and stare at the wall. When you think one minute has gone by, look down at the watch again. Were you on the short side of the minute or did you go beyond it? If so, by how many seconds?

Practice a few times to become more precise. Keep track of your score on paper (see sample below). Under "First Try," "Second Try," "Third Try," enter the number of seconds of clock time that you felt was a minute. In a short while you will discover that you can predict a minute's time quite accurately.

If, after three tries, you don't improve, try counting to yourself as you stare at the wall. This may help you be more precise. Enter those results. Then try again without counting. Next, see if you can estimate a minute's time as well while reading from a book. Again enter your score. Finally, sit somewhere in the dark and try to estimate a minute. See if you can do just as well under those conditions.

Once you become adept at inner clocking, see if you can train a friend to become more precise at judging the passage of clock time.

	First Try	Second Try	Third Try
Staring at the wall			
Counting to myself			
Reading			
Sitting in the dark			

2. SLEEP CLOCK

PREPARATION

The purpose of this exercise is to see how good your sleeping brain is at judging time.

THE EXERCISE

Immediately upon waking up in the morning, before looking at any clock or watch, write down what time you think it is. Then look at the clock and see what it says. How close were you?

If you tend to wake up during the night, try the exercise then, writing down the time you think it is, then turning on the light to see what the clock says. Do this over several nights for comparison. For a change, you may also do this exercise at various moments during the day, guessing what hour it is, then checking a clock or watch.

Date	Day or Night	Time I Thought It Was	Clock Time

3. BUILT-IN ALARM

PREPARATION

This exercise is designed to determine whether your internal clock can serve as an alarm clock. You'll need (1) a clock or watch, and (2) pencil and paper.

THE EXERCISE

Just before dropping off to sleep at night, decide on a specific time when you want to wake up. Be exact, and repeat the time to yourself a couple of times. Visualize a clock dial, with the hands pointing to the designated time. Think of the time as you go to sleep.

The moment you wake up in the morning, look at the clock.

How close were you?

Try this exercise over a few nights, and note your improvement.

Date	Time Expected	Actual Time Awakening

4. PULSE TIMING

PREPARATION

The pulse in blood vessels comes from the beating of the heart. The heartbeat is a biological rhythm common to all animals, but its rate differs in various animals. Very small animals such as sparrows and mice have heartbeats so fast that they can be counted only with a recording device. Children's pulses beat faster than grown-ups'.

Your heartbeat speeds up when you exercise or when you are excited or frightened. It follows a regular daily cycle, too. From the moment you wake up in the morning, through midday and through evening, your pulse changes a little in a regular daily rhythm. See if you can make careful measurements of your own pulse, and find this daily rhythm of your heart. You will need (1) a stop watch, and (2) pencil and paper for this exercise.

THE EXERCISE

Set the stop watch for one minute and hold it in your left hand. With the tips of the third and fourth fingers of the right hand feel the pulse on your left wrist. You can find it by first locating the hard cord under the skin that is a major tendon to your hand. Run the tips of your third and fourth fingers up and down this tendon lightly. Feel where it disappears into the hand near the thumb. Then let your fingertips slide off the tendon onto the left side of it, and there you should feel the thump of your pulse. If you don't feel it, press just a little harder and move your fingertips around slowly until you do feel it.

When you know you can count the pulse, start the watch and begin counting. You may have to attempt the count several times before you are practiced enough to keep it up a full minute.

Every day for at least five days take your pulse as soon as you wake up and before you get out of bed. Check it again around noon before eating lunch, and again after dinner or before you go to bed. Keep a chart of your results.

	PULSE RECORD		
	MORNING *pulses/minute*	*NOON* *pulses/minute*	*NIGHT* *pulses/minute*
Day 1.			
Day 2.			
Day 3.			
Day 4.			
Day 5.			

When you think you have kept the chart for a sufficient number of days, average out each column by adding it up and dividing the result by the number of days in the column.

When is your pulse highest, and when is it lowest — morning, noon, or night? Judging by your results, when do you think you have the most adrenalin in your blood?

5. MOOD CHART

PREPARATION

Some days you feel great and some days you just seem to drag around, sad and depressed, right? Everybody is like this. We all have up days and down days and many in-between days. Now the question is: do these moods come on because of things that happen to us or because of a pattern within us?

THE EXERCISE

Keep track for at least two months of how you feel every day. A good way is to keep this book next to your bed and at night write down how you have felt most of the day. Rate yourself on a scale. Give yourself plus 5 when you're really high — feeling magnificent, exuberant, thinking the world is a great place to be. Mark plus 2 or 3 for medium happiness. Minus 5 would be the score when you're feeling miserable — sad and mad at the whole stupid, horrible world. Each day rate your mood somewhere between plus 5 and minus 5. If there is some special reason that you think might affect your mood, such as being in bed with a 104-degree fever, or receiving a million dollars from an unknown benefactor, mark that down too.

Then chart out your results by putting a dot at the proper level for each day and draw a line from one dot to another. Study the chart. Do your moods seem to follow any pattern or not?

This information will be useful because, as you will learn in the following pages, your mood can be markedly affected by your sleep and dreams.

DAYS

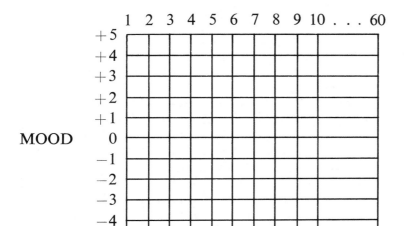

GETTING READY

Sleep time can be a sensuous time and the time before it can be a winding down, a gradual relaxation of your body, an easing of tensions to rid yourself of the cares of the day and to prepare for the renewal of the night.

Enjoy the relaxation and the preparation for sleep. Don't spend the minutes before bed wrestling with a problem or arguing. Sit in front of the fire and think over the day. Luxuriate in a warm bath, letting the steam soothe the pains of the day's pressures. Lie back and listen to music. Read. Talk to someone you love.

It's best to fall asleep on the crest of sleepiness, not rushing it and not putting it off. So try to arrange your evening accordingly, doing quiet things until that sleepy feeling hits you. Then stretch and yawn a few times, think of your warm, safe, comfortable, luxurious, marvelous bed. And head straight for it.

Crawl in, snuggle down, and drift away to the pleasant dreams you deserve.

6. DEEP WATER

PREPARATION

A bath can be more than just a means of getting clean. To get the most from it, make your bath a leisurely one.

Fill the tub with water that is relaxingly warm, but not so hot that it wilts you. Add some bath oil for an extra touch.

THE EXERCISE

Lie quietly in the deep water and luxuriate in the warmth. Wash slowly and enjoy it, stretching your muscles. Massage out the kinks and feel the tensions recede.

After your bath, stretch out between clean sheets and appreciate how well you feel, how ready for a good night's sleep.

Concentration

Any mental occupation without a personal emotional undertone to which you can direct your mind and that you can concentrate on, sometimes for five minutes, at other times perhaps considerably longer, will intercept the circuit of your unpleasant thoughts or painful moods.

Margaret Steger

Using Suggestion

Suggestion is of particular value when it is a present-day difficulty which is causing the anxiety, depression or sleeplessness, and which the patient finds himself incapable of dealing with. He needs support, and suggestion provides the temporary splint to tide him over the difficulty till he can carry on for himself.

J. A. Hadfield

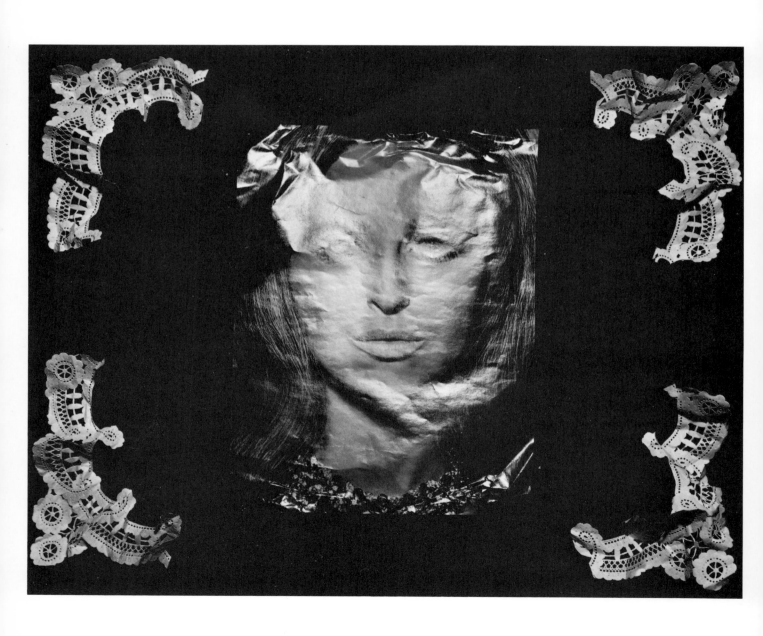

164

7. MASSAGE

PREPARATION

An excellent way to get yourself into the proper frame of mind for a good night's sleep is to have a massage.

Of course, the best massages are administered by the loving hands of husband, wife, or friend — or by a professional masseur or masseuse. But if you lack a suitable partner, there are also valuable massage techniques which you can apply to yourself.

A facial massage is easy to administer to oneself and has often been used successfully to conquer insomnia.

THE EXERCISE

Lying on your bed, close your eyes. Put both hands lightly over your face and with your middle fingers stroke your forehead gently in a steady, slow, circular movement.

Slide your hands down a little and repeat the circular movement over your eyelids and eye sockets.

Slide your hands down still further, place the middle fingers at the corners of your mouth and stroke upward in light circular movements, all the way up to the temples.

Repeat each of these movements a few times, until you feel relaxed and ready to drop off to sleep.

Inducing Sleep

Any form of continued and monotonous stimulus will induce tiredness and sleep.

Pavlov

8. SLEEP IMPROVERS

PREPARATION

One way to decrease the quantity of sleep you need may be to improve the quality of the sleep you get. To this end, you must first rid yourself of the sleep-stealers.

THE EXERCISE

First of all, free yourself from stress, tension, depression, guilt, anger, frustration, and from the compulsion of recapitulating over and over all those things you should have said and didn't.

Some people need absolute silence and darkness in order to sleep. If you are one of them, eliminate as much noise as possible by means of carpeting, drapes, and any other sound-conditioning you can afford.

One man who sleeps during the day has black walls, heavy blinds on the windows, and black drapes. In addition, he puts ear-plugs in his ears and a sleep mask over his eyes. He sleeps through anything. Others swear by a steady "white" noise — a ticking clock, the sound of the surf, or the gentle patter of rain.

But even if you like to go to sleep with sound, don't play the radio all night. The National Research Council of Canada says that the noise level of a radio, even when tuned very low, can disturb a sleeper without actually waking him by keeping him from a deep sleep and disrupting his dreams. If you like music to go to sleep by, have it turn off automatically after a short time.

A Dry Brain Never Sleeps Well

Many cannot sleep for witches and fascinations. . . . But the ordinary causes are heat and dryness, which must first be removed: a hot and dry brain never sleeps well: grief, fears, cares, expectations, anxieties . . . and all violent perturbations of the mind must in some sort be qualified before we can hope for any good repose. He that sleeps in the day time, or is in suspense, fear . . . or goes to bed upon a full stomach may never hope for a quiet rest in the night.

Robert Burton

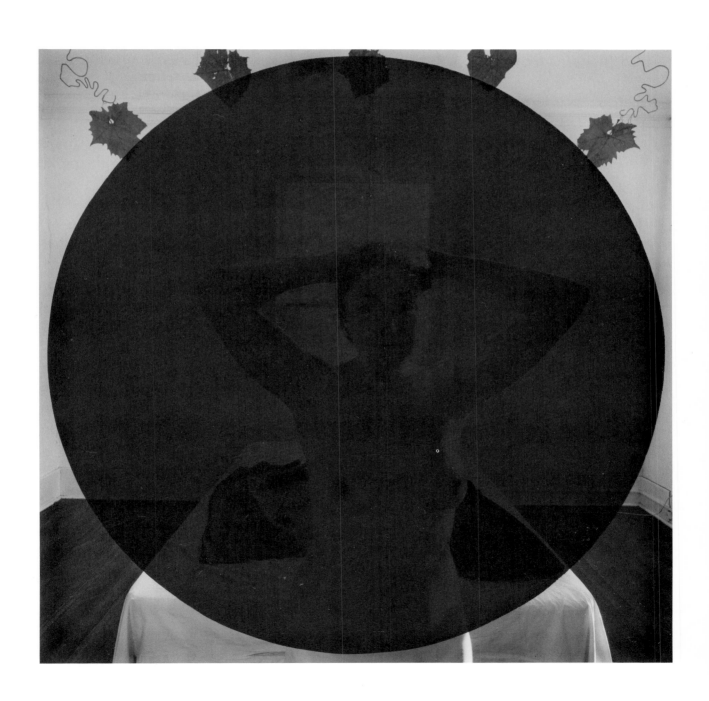

9. NIGHT FOOD

PREPARATION

The sleep experts may say it's okay to snack before bedtime. But there are also those middle-of-the-night awakenings with the uncontrollable urges to raid the refrigerator. Insomniacs are given to food cravings, usually in the darkest hour of the night.

There are several theories to explain these nocturnal cravings, such as that we produce tensions from anxious dreams and try to ease them through food, or that the insomniac may not produce enough growth hormone and may need more protein at night when most growth hormone is released.

THE EXERCISE

Try milk at bedtime. It works for a good many people — and not just by suggestion. Much more likely, it works because milk contains the amino acids that break down to make serotonin — one of the chemicals involved in sleep chemistry. Unless you are allergic to it (and a surprising number of adults are), try a glass of lukewarm milk the next time you feel the need of a little something to help you across the sleep threshold. If milk isn't strong enough, and your figure can afford it, have a glass of beer instead. In any case, avoid stimulants such as coffee, tea, or colas, unless you are (1) very used to them, or (2) one of the oddballs on whom they have a paradoxical soporific effect.

NOTE

How can you fulfill the urge to eat so you can get back to sleep and still not get fat?

Here are some foods to have handy in the refrigerator that will assuage your hunger without expanding your waist: celery, carrot sticks, lettuce, sliced green peppers, raw cauliflower and cabbage, cottage cheese, lean meat, skim milk, juices, apples, strawberries, tangerines, dietetic jello and puddings.

About Late Night Suppers

If ever I ate a good supper at night,
I dream'd of the devil,
and wak'd in a fright.

Christopher Anstey

From Fumes and Humors

All Dreams, as in old Gallen I have read,
Are from Repletion and Complexion
bred;
From rising Fumes of indigested Food,
And noxious Humors that infect the
Blood.

John Dryden

10. ROUTINE

PREPARATION

Sticking to a routine trains your body to follow a regular rhythm. If you go to bed at the same hour every night, your inner biological clock is strengthened in maintaining a regular rhythm for your body to follow.

THE EXERCISE

Try to determine the best sleep pattern for you. On two or three days when you have no important plans, forget about schedules, and simply do what you want to do, when you want to do it. But keep a record of your activities — especially of the times when you feel sleepy, when you go to sleep, and when you wake up. Do this for several days in a row and over several different weeks. From this record, your natural pattern will gradually emerge. When you have pinpointed it, try to accommodate your schedule to it. It often helps people to have a certain routine of things to do as they get ready for bed. If you can fall into bed and sleep no matter what — fine. But if you have difficulty falling asleep, determine the things that make you feel relaxed and then work them into a regular pre-bedtime routine. Whatever it is — reading a book, taking a bath, brushing your hair — do it every night to start your mind and body on the road to relaxation.

If you tend to worry about whether everything is taken care of after you get into bed, make a checklist then. Go down the list and take care of the items one by one. Make sure the door is locked, the cat is out, the lights are out, and there's nobody under the bed. Then read through the list once more to assure yourself that absolutely everything is done, turn out the light, and fall asleep without nagging worries.

If you establish and follow such a routine long enough, you will eventually find yourself growing sleepy automatically at that time.

Other Ways to Sleep

Although many animals lie down to sleep, some of them sit in trees. Certain birds sleep standing on one leg, others while hanging from branches or clinging to walls. Some creatures sleep while flying or while swimming in circles.

A sleep fact

Without Any Drugs

By exercising, by increasing activity, or by developing better habits around the time of sleep, you can get over a mild degree of insomnia without any drugs.

Dr. Anthony Kales

A British Psychologist Comments

A man may choose to be a milkman because he likes to get up at 4 a.m., not because he has trained himself to wake early.

Edward Stonehill

II. BED AND PILLOWS

PREPARATION

According to the Islamic religion, only kings may sleep on the right side; wise men on the left; and saints on their backs. The devil sleeps on his stomach. Doesn't leave much room for the rest of us.

Folklore says those with heart or liver trouble should sleep with a pillow on one side, and with their knees bent. Those with problems of gas, it is said, should sleep on their stomach. Studies show that people who usually assume the same position when they go to bed fall asleep more easily, so find the way you like to sleep and burrow in.

Learning to Sleep

Infants in the early weeks of life seem to be incapable of sustaining a long period of sleep or a very long period of wakefulness. As they mature, they acquire the ability to do both.

Dr. A. H. Parmelee, Jr.

THE EXERCISE

Check the simple things. Maybe you need a new mattress. Make sure your pillow is right for you, that your sheets are fresh, and your blanket or comforter neither too light nor too heavy. Make sure your bedroom isn't too hot or cold. Studies indicate that most people sleep best in a room with temperature between 60 and 65 degrees. Wear loose-fitting bedclothes, or none, whichever makes you comfortable.

If you have back trouble, you should always sleep on a firm mattress. In fact, if your back trouble is chronic and you are in a hotel bed with a soft mattress, it will pay to fold a bedspread and put it over the mattress, or to put an extra pillow under your hips.

Dr. Arthur Michele in his book *Orthotherapy* recommends that persons with low-back pain use a bed board of ¾-inch plywood, cut to one inch less than the dimensions of the mattress. Place it between the box spring and the mattress for better support.

If you tend to get a stiff neck, try sleeping with a small soft pillow to avoid unusual angles or stress on the neck during sleep. And sleep on your back or on your side — not on your stomach with your head and neck twisted to one side.

Do You Sleep on Your Back?

Twice as many women sleep on their stomach as men. Most men sleep on their back; in fact, four times more men than women favor that position.

A sleep fact

Bedroom Companions

Eskimo children nestle between their parents at night in the single-room igloos. African bush children cuddle in their parents' arms in the big sleeping circle around the campfire. Among Norsemen everyone — sometimes as many as a dozen families — slept in the same communal room.

Even in western countries the idea that a child should sleep in his own room is relatively new. Until recently most children, because of large families, had some bedroom companions.

A sleep fact

12. RITUALS

PREPARATION

Many famous people have been known for their special rituals for going to sleep. Alexander Dumas was advised to eat an apple — at 7 A.M., under the Arc de Triomphe. After getting up early and walking all the way across Paris in the crisp morning air, even before his regular working day began, he had little trouble falling asleep at night.

Marcel Proust was so bothered by noise that he lined his bedroom with cork, and when he traveled he always rented the rooms on either side of the one he occupied to protect himself against noisy neighbors.

Charles Dickens placed his hotel beds in such a manner that his head faced north and his feet south because he thought it would make the electromagnetic currents flow correctly through his body.

Madame Chiang Kai-Shek always takes her own sheets with her when she travels — even to the White House, it is said.

Catherine II used to have her hair brushed till she fell asleep.

THE EXERCISE

Take a few minutes to list, in your mind or on paper, the things that help you relax. It may be a nightly prayer, or counting sheep, or drinking hot milk, or hugging a teddy bear, or having a light on in the closet, or wearing purple pajamas.

Once you discover what helps, make a ritual of it. Do it religiously, and allow yourself to relax as you carry it out.

It's Not Enough

It's not enough to sleep — sleep must be organized!

George Mikes

On the Right Side of the Bed

Getting up on the right side of the bed each morning is seldom an accident, it's a planned procedure.

Don Bingham

DROPPING OFF

Relaxation is vital for entering sleep, and it also helps you to take full advantage of your sleep and dream states. The following are exercises to induce relaxation.

13. SLEEP TALK

PREPARATION

Usually, simply settling in bed and letting your mind roam will be relaxing enough to bring about sleep, but if you have difficulty, you might talk yourself into a state of relaxation with a sleep-talk. Repeating instructions to relax is helpful to many people.

THE EXERCISE

Speaking slowly and simply, you might try saying something like this to yourself:

> My eyelids are growing heavy,
> growing heavier and heavier.
> My whole body
> is becoming very relaxed.
> I am relaxing
> more and more,
> deeper . . . and deeper . . .
> Eyelids heavy . . .
> heavier . . . and heavier.
> I am completely relaxed now,
> from the top of my head . . .
> all the way
> to the tips of my toes.
> I am getting sleepier and sleepier . . .
> Sleepier and sleepier . . .

NOTE

Those who require a much longer sleep-talk may improvise other words to say to themselves. Others will discover that they need to repeat this exercise over five or six nights before the inner mind becomes accustomed to the words as a relaxation technique.

Alice Dozing Off

And here Alice began to get rather sleepy, and went on saying to herself, in a dreamy sort of way, "Do cats eat bats? Do cats eat bats?" and sometimes "Do bats eat cats?" for, you see, as she couldn't answer either question, it didn't much matter which way she put it. She felt that she was dozing off, and had just begun to dream that she was walking hand in hand with Dinah, and was saying to her, very earnestly, "Now, Dinah, tell me the truth: did you ever eat a bat?" when suddenly, thump! thump! down she came upon a heap of sticks and dry leaves, and the fall was over.

Lewis Carroll
Through the Looking Glass

Afraid of the Dark

Do you know what the stars are, Mother?
They're the lights God puts out
So I won't be afraid
Of the dark

"He told me that just before he went to sleep," she confided . . .

"He is confessing something to you," I said. "He is too much of a proud man to admit in other language that he is afraid of the dark. If you asked him about it — and you must not, if you wish to preserve these confidences — he would probably deny it. But he is telling you, just the same. When he speaks thus in his native language it is important. Some children pass through this fear without harm; to others it is a memory that persists to defeat them later in life. So if he needs you near just now, your voice in the next room or a distant light for protection, see to it."

Hughes Mearns

175

14. RELAXING WITH YOGA

PREPARATION

People young and old have found yoga exercises helpful for meditation, but yoga techniques can also aid people preparing for sleep. Rachel Carr, in her recent book *Yoga for All Ages,* describes the following simple steps to encourage relaxation.

THE EXERCISE

"The first phase in relaxing is to remove or loosen any tight clothing. Then lie on your back with your arms and legs loosely apart. Close your eyes and stretch out to full length. Breathe in deeply (through the nose) and raise your arms over your head. Hold your breath and stretch from head to toe like a cat, tensing all muscles. Then let go and exhale slowly (again through the nose), while you drop your arms limply forward and down. This method of stretching is a good way to wake yourself up in the mornings and to feel more alert when you wish.

"The second step to complete relaxation is to let your imagination take over. As you lie limply at ease, feel as if you are sinking, slowly sinking. Take a long, deep breath and imagine that a flow of energy is saturating your body. Exhale quietly, releasing your breath very slowly.

"Then relax your muscles. Starting with your feet, tense them, and let go. Bend your toes down, stretch each one and let go. Now concentrate on each toe and feel it becoming limp. Let your thoughts move gradually to relax the insteps, heels, calves, knees, and thighs until your legs feel loose and free. Slowly bend your right knee, then let it move back to its relaxed position. Now bend and relax your left knee in the same way. Think of waves of relaxation

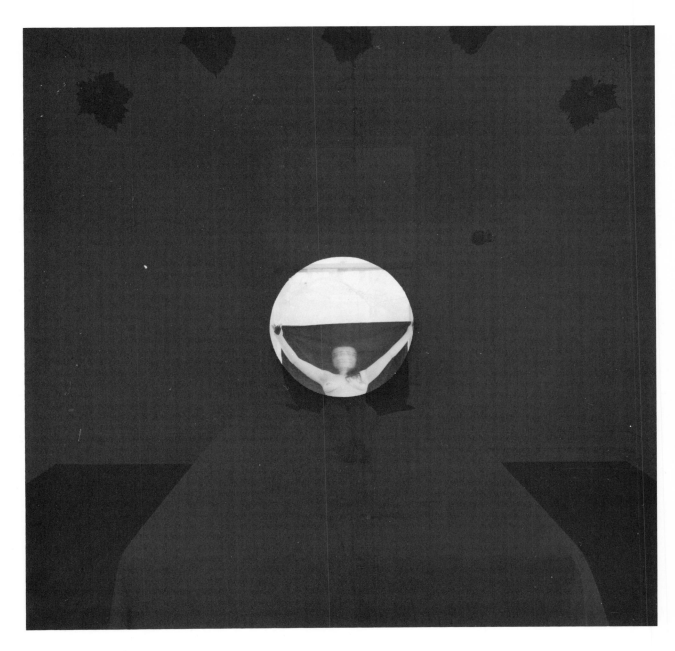

spreading into your thighs, abdomen, chest, and shoulders; then down into your spine and the small of your back. Feel a tingling sensation as the muscles begin to loosen. Now let your arms and hands become limp. Relax your fingers one by one. Close and open your fists just to feel how relaxed your hands have become.

"Next direct your mind to your facial muscles, which we never think of relaxing. Let your jaw sag with lips slightly parted so that your teeth are not clenched. Yawn and stretch the facial muscles. Then feel a loosening of your scalp. Let your eyes sink back into their sockets, resting them in a sea of black silence. The feeling of relaxation is gradually overtaking your whole body. Feel that you are slowly melting away until you are light as air.

"Now lie still and become conscious of the steady, slow beating of your heart. Observe your breath as it flows in and out with quiet rhythmic control. Then breathe in deeply and imagine that you are absorbing the forces of energy around you. The inner vibrations of your body are responding to the fresh intake of oxygen. As you breathe out, feel the loosening of tension knots.

"Let your mind play steadily on the quiet flow of the breath. Feel that you are dissolving in a state of peace all around you, without clinging to any thoughts. You have now moved into a sphere of serenity, and you are no longer confined within your body. These brief moments of mental refuge will give the mind a rest and induce a mood of tranquility."

15. COUNTING

PREPARATION

For centuries, slow monotonous counting has been used as a way of inducing sleep. Counting sheep is perhaps the most traditional form. The present exercise uses a new variation.

THE EXERCISE

Close your eyes and relax your body as completely as you can, from the top of your head to your toes. Let yourself sink deeper and deeper into this state of relaxation, mentally and physically. Now tell yourself that you will count slowly from ten down to zero. As you do this, visualize the numbers in a downward progression, as if each successive number were standing one step lower on a staircase. Tell yourself that when you have reached zero you will be asleep. Feel the relaxation spreading throughout every muscle and nerve of your body as you count.

NOTE

Some people like to count in a forward direction, from one to ten. They might pretend that they are slowly drawing each number on a huge blackboard in their mind, or across a giant sky, moving their eyes slowly, outlining the numbers as they draw. Do a "2" twice, drawing it slowly, very slowly, and as large as possible. Draw a "3" three times, and so on. Continue until sleep takes over.

One Needs More Rest

I haven't been to sleep for over a year. That's why I go to bed early. One needs more rest if one doesn't sleep.

Evelyn Waugh
Decline and Fall

180

181

16. CREATING PICTURES

PREPARATION

Often before bedtime, especially after a busy day, the mind is jumping from thought to thought, muscles are twitching and eager nerves can't seem to settle down. Concentrating on an imaginary scene, especially a pleasant and restful one, can help relax mind, muscles and nerves. This exercise suggests a variety of pictures you can create.

THE EXERCISE

Create a picture in your mind. If it is a simple object, study every line of it, appreciating the graceful curves and the texture and feel of it. Or picture one color in a variety of patterns and hues, continually blending and changing.

You may even want to picture an entire scene with a quiet mood: a soft, silent, white-covered snow scene, perhaps with fluffy snowflakes falling slowly and steadily; or a pastoral painting of greens and blues, with cows and horses slowly grazing along a meadow. Picturing peaceful scenes will generally make it possible to erase tense thoughts left over from the day.

One of the best ways to relax is to think of downward movement. Picture yourself floating down, down like a feather, or imagine going down a staircase or riding down an elevator. The lower you go, the deeper you go into relaxation and sleep.

Or imagine yourself floating on a cloud, or in a boat, drifting quietly in the sun. Or feel yourself floating on the surface of the water in a large swimming pool, comfortably immersed in warm water, carried by the

soothing motion of the waves, listening to the gentle
sound of the water surrounding you and supporting
you.

Stay with your picture, get completely involved in it
until you feel yourself completely relaxed.

17. BREATHING TO SLEEP

PREPARATION

Breathing exercises are excellent sleep inducers. While you're lying in bed, try this exercise:

THE EXERCISE

Breathe out through the mouth. Then take in a deep breath through the nose, first pushing out your abdomen to fill up with air, then pulling in. Hold your breath five to ten seconds, then exhale through your nose as slowly as you can while contracting your abdomen. Wait a couple of seconds, then repeat the process.

NOTE

While doing this exercise, some people like to place a hand over their abdomen, imagining a balloon inside inflating and deflating with each breath.

Children may enjoy mentally visualizing how high they can blow the balloon, how long they can hold it full-blown, or how slowly they can "let the air out."

18. RIGHT AND LEFT BREATHING

PREPARATION

An excellent yoga exercise to do before bedtime is a breathing technique in which the breath flows in and out of the nostrils alternatingly.

To clear your nose at the beginning of the exercise, press your right thumb on the right nostril and forcefully inhale and exhale through the left nostril 15 to 20 times. Then close the left nostril with the fourth finger and repeat the same deep forceful breathing through the right nostril.

THE EXERCISE

Sit in a meditative yoga posture. Press your right thumb on your right nostril. Inhale deeply and smoothly through the left nostril to the count of 5 seconds. Close the left nostril with the fourth finger. Release your thumb and slowly exhale through the right nostril to the count of 10 seconds.

Without releasing the finger from the left nostril, inhale through the right nostril to the count of 5 seconds. Close your right nostril with your thumb, at the same time releasing the left nostril and exhale to the count of 10 seconds.

This is one round of alternating breathing. Practice until you are able to do three rounds without stopping, allowing the breath to flow steadily into and out of the nostrils. Then increase the time for inhaling from 5 seconds to 6 seconds, and the time for exhaling to 12 seconds. Later increase the counts to 7 for inhaling and 14 for exhaling, and then to 8 for inhaling and 16 for exhaling.

To Neutralize Your Mind

The ability to neutralize one's mind consists of directing one's thoughts deliberately toward subjects which have no emotional impact at all and to concentrate on them. This presupposes adequate mental-emotional self-direction and the ability to concentrate.

Margaret Steger

NOTE

Perform this exercise on or near your bed, so that
when you feel relaxed, you can slide between the
sheets with minimal effort.

19. NEW AIR

PREPARATION

Some people enjoy exercising before they go to bed. Others simply like to renew the air in their lungs for a good night's rest.

If you have been inside or at a desk job all day, it may help to take a walk before you turn in.

If walking is too much exercise, try standing in front of an open window drawing some deep breaths. Or try one of the following breathing techniques.

EXERCISE

1. Lie on your back in bed with your legs stretched out and your arms at your side, palms up. Breathe in gently through your nose, out through your mouth. Then breathe with your mouth wide open. Then yawn as deeply as you can. Repeat this cycle until you fall asleep.

2. Lie on your back with your knees together and drawn up toward your chest, and one hand resting over your chest. This should involve no straining or tension. Complete relaxation is essential. As the

The Motivation of Pleasure

Pleasure provides the motivation and energy for the creative process, which in turn increases the pleasure and joy of living. With pleasure, life is a creative adventure; without pleasure, it is a struggle for survival.

Alexander Lowen

object of the exercise is to empty the lungs, begin with a short sniff through the nose followed by a long expiration through the mouth, making an "f" or "s" sound with the lips and teeth.

Exhale slowly while gently "sinking" the chest as much as possible and then the upper part of the abdomen. Following expiration, the fingers rest lightly on the upper abdomen or lower front ends of the ribs.

Relax the upper part of the abdomen so that it and the lower chest are felt to expand slightly while air is inhaled through the nose, quickly but silently. The chest is not raised. Repeat this exercise eight to sixteen times.

3. Lying flat in bed, place a medium-sized book or weight on your abdomen just below the ribs. The book thus rests on your diaphragm, and rises and falls gently as you inhale and exhale.

Make the stomach push the weight upward when breathing in, let it fall back when breathing out. Over a period of time, the additional weight will strengthen your diaphragm.

For All the Thrones

**What a delightful thing rest is!
The bed has become a place of luxury to me.
I would not exchange it for all the thrones in the world.**

Napoleon Bonaparte

Get Rid of Strain

There may be strain to start with, but it is getting rid of strain, both physical and mental, which constitutes relaxation, or blankness, of the conscious mind. Practice will teach you what this state is, and after a while you can achieve it without strain.

Mrs. Upton Sinclair

189

20. UNTENSING

PREPARATION

The following techniques are designed to encourage muscle relaxation and to counteract tenseness.

THE EXERCISES

Straight-Leg Raising. Lie on your back, a small pillow under your head. Keeping the knee straight, raise one leg from the floor or bed until it reaches about a 45-degree angle. Then lower the leg. Repeat with the other leg. Repeat this exercise several times, slowly raising first one leg and then the other, exhaling as you raise the leg and inhaling as you lower it.

Head and Shoulder Raising. Still lying on your back, raise head and shoulders off the floor or bed. Exhale while raising them and inhale while lowering them to the original position.

Side Expansion Breathing. This exercise may be done lying on your back or sitting with your back against a support. Place your hands over your rib cage with the little fingers resting on the lowest ribs. Keep the shoulders down throughout the exercise.

Begin with a short sniff through the nose. Breathe out slowly through the mouth, first sinking the chest as much as possible, then the lower ribs, and, finally, squeezing the ribs to help expel the air from the lungs. Repeat eight to sixteen times, resting when necessary. This exercise may be modified by the use of a belt instead of the hands for pressure over the lower ribs. The loose ends of the belt are grasped with the hands and pulled together, exerting an even compression on the lower ribs.

The Animal that Worries

Man has his disturbances in sleep, not because of danger as he sleeps, but because he is the one animal that broods over the past and worries about the future.

Dr. Heinz Hediger

190

Forward Bending. Sit with arms relaxed at the sides. Breathe out slowly while dropping your head. Sink your chest, and bend forward until your head is above or between your knees. Contract the abdominal muscles firmly during the last part of the bending.

Breathe in gradually while raising the body so that your hips straighten first, followed by the back, shoulders, neck, and finally the head.

Pleasure Without Anxiety

Pleasure cannot be given unless the senses are in a state of accepting rather than taking, and for this reason they must not be, as it were, paralyzed and rigidified by the anxiety to get something out of the object.

Alan W. Watts

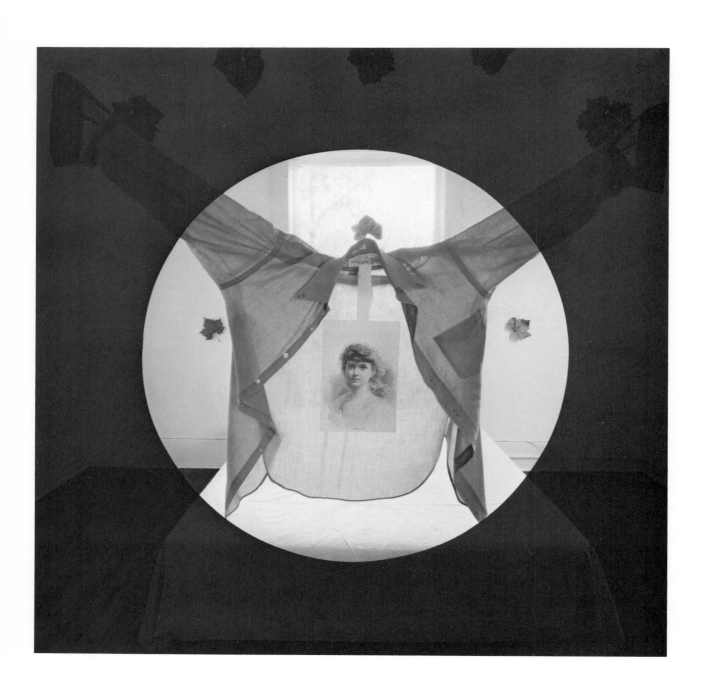

DREAMWORLDS

Being at Ease with Dreams

In learning to use our sleep and dreams, it is important that we think of them as a natural part of ourselves. Even dreams that seem abnormal or fearful, or involve ESP, should not give reason for being frightened.

"Take them in stride as something that is perfectly natural," says Dr. Stanley Krippner. "Dreams of the future, of other people's thoughts, and of distant events do seem to occur. We don't know why this happens or how this happens. Nevertheless, these events are apparently part of the life process — not a bizarre, abnormal peculiarity that should be feared or suppressed."

Learn to be conscious of your various stages of sleep. Feel yourself dropping off to sleep, be aware of the images and thoughts wandering through your mind at that time.

Consider your emotions and feelings in relation to sleep. Do you feel relaxed or tense? What sort of things run through your mind when you wake up in the middle of the night? What is your state of mind as you come through the lighter stages and wake up to the world again in the morning?

One of the principles of Zen teaching is based upon awakening perception to the core of one's being by inward listening. Learn to listen to your inner being in sleep and dreams; it will pay off in greater self-awareness during your waking hours.

New Realms of Experience

In forming a bridge between body and mind, dreams may be used as a springboard from which man can leap to new realms of experience lying outside his normal state of consciousness and enlarge his vision not only of himself, but also of the universe in which he lives.

Dr. Ann Faraday

The Relevance of Dreams

It is remarkable that contemporary psychology has so insistently ignored dreams. Most introductory psychology textbooks contain no mention of dreams whatever, nor are the texts used in advanced course work much better. Despite the apparent relevance of dreams for understanding personality, only a few universities offer course work on this subject.

Dr. Robert L. Van de Castle

Pray for a Dream

We shall pray for a dream, even as Homer, perchance, prayed. And if you are worthy, the god far away is present with you. Nay, even what time the god sets little store on these matters, he comes to your side if only you are asleep; and this is the whole system of the initiation. In it no one has ever yet lamented his poverty, on the ground that thus he had less possessions than the rich.

Synesius of Cyrene

21. A DREAM WATCHER'S GUIDE

PREPARATION

Much can be learned from observing not only our own sleep but also that of others. The next time you wake up next to the person you love, listen to the pattern of breathing, look at his or her face in repose, see if you can observe any eye movement beneath the closed lids. If so, you know that the sleeper is dreaming. Now try to imagine what the dream mood might be . . . does the facial expression mirror a happy dream or an anxious one — or even a nightmare?

You can also watch an animal sleeping.

THE EXERCISE

First note the way your pet animal approaches sleep. Cats and dogs usually turn several times on the sleeping area, in a circular motion, before settling down and closing their eyes.

Slow-wave sleep sets in first. Note that respiration is regular and fairly slow. The animal is still and quiet, almost motionless. After 10 or 20 minutes, the first REM, or paradoxical, sleep period begins. Now you can see the eyes moving under the eyelids, which may be closed or partly open. Breathing becomes irregular, rapid and shallow; sometimes the animal may even seem to hold its breath. This is the period of sleep when the ears and whiskers, or even the whole face, may twitch. Sometimes the paws make jerky movements as if the animal were actually running in his sleep. There is no doubt that it is dreaming.

Sometimes a child, even an infant, will show signs of facial movements and twitching just as observed in animals. Or the infant may make sucking movements. These, too, are signs of REM sleep.

Affecting Dreams

External stimuli can have an effect on dreams. Cologne may make you dream you are in a perfume shop, water splashed on you may make you dream of rain or a waterfall, the sound of a buzzer may make you dream of a telephone ringing.

A sleep fact

Dreams Take Just As Long

Dreams are not encapsulated into a few seconds as was previously thought. Some evidence points to the fact that action in a dream takes just as long as it would for the same action to take place in daytime reality.

A sleep fact

22. CATCHING A DREAM

PREPARATION

One person interested in dream research described dreams as "cinema verité" of the unconscious. Whether we analyze dreams to probe deep thoughts and feelings, creatively adapt them for artistic expression and problem-solving, or simply enjoy them as mind-adventures, they should be seen, heard, and welcomed to the ordinary world.

But to analyze a dream or even just to enjoy it, you must first remember it. Since most of us forget most of our dreams, here are a number of hints for catching your dreams before they are lost forever.

THE EXERCISE

1. Keep pen and paper, or a tape recorder, by your bed.

2. Have a dim light handy that you can switch on from the bed.

3. Before falling asleep, tell yourself several times, "I will remember a dream tonight."

4. If after a few nights you do not wake up spontaneously, set an alarm clock for about two hours after you go to bed, or if you don't want to awaken early in the night, set the alarm for early morning.

5. When you wake up, immediately think of what you were dreaming, switch on the light, and write down or dictate into a tape recorder the dream with as many details as you can remember.

6. Add as many associations as you can: what you think the dream may mean, events of the day or from the past that may have sparked it, your feelings both during and after the dream.

Remembering Your Dreams

How long do people remember their dreams? Usually not long at all. They dream several dreams every night, but seldom remember them in the morning. It seems to depend on whether they wake up immediately after the dreams. In the laboratory, if awakened right at the end of an REM period, subjects will remember the dream they just had. Awaken them just a few minutes later and the dream will have already disappeared, their mind left a blank.

A sleep fact

A Vivid REM Dream

I had rather an unpleasant dream the other night. I dreamt that I was in a future State Department of Dentistry and that I sat in a chair, when a presiding official looked at my teeth and decided what was to be done. Then without a moment's delay a Robot dentist sat in front of me and set to work. He was mechanically efficient, but, of course, he paid not the slightest attention to any sense of pain or discomfort that occurred in the course of his operations. I was told, however, that if I left him, my teeth would not be attended to by the State or anyone else.

E. S. P. Haynes

A Hidden Treasure

I was a hidden treasure, I yearned to be known.

Ibn' Arabi

Your Brothers' Dreams

Respect your brothers' dreams.

American Indian proverb

Drinking Licence

. . . I dreamed of finding myself in a country where no man was allowed to drink beer or wine promiscuously and had to swear eternal fidelity to some particular beer or wine. In my dream I was much alarmed because some enterprising policeman had discovered a bottle of claret up my chimney when I had a licence to drink nothing but Moselle.

E. S. P. Hayes

7. If you awaken in the morning with a dream, write it down or record it while still in bed.

8. Keep your dreams and their interpretations together in a looseleaf notebook, with each page dated for easy reference.

23. DREAM NOTES

PREPARATION

Too often we are unaware of our inner feelings, unaware of the hidden aspects of our personalities, out of touch with our own unconscious emotions.

We can help get in touch with ourselves and some of our deepest feelings by using our dreams. Many psychiatrists say that we might enjoy better mental health if we could develop more self-awareness by learning to recall, understand and act upon our dreams. We can do this by remembering our dreams, writing them down, analyzing them, and facing them squarely.

Dr. Harry Gershman, Dean of the American Institute for Psychoanalysis of the Karen Horney Psychoanalytic Center, says the dream can reveal a person's basic feelings, values, philosophy and methods of coping with his emotional problems.

Dr. Gershman and Dr. Ann Faraday believe in the value of interpreting one's own dreams with or without professional assistance. However, they caution that not every dream has great meaning. Some dreams can lead to deep insights, but others can be as silly and trivial as some of our daytime thoughts.

What about symbols in dreams? How do you go about interpreting them? Psychoanalysts, in general, no longer believe in universal symbols that mean the same thing for everybody; they believe that the meaning of symbols is individual and personal, depending upon one's life experiences. A box in one person's dream may mean something completely different from a box in another person's dream. You need to

196

think your dream through and consider what some of the symbolism might mean for you. Equally important as content is the *mood* of the dream, and the emotions you felt while dreaming it.

Dr. Stanley Krippner advises that you also look for word-plays that may explain some dream images. He tells, for example, of a man who dreamed of bows and arrows, then later of his wife putting a bow tie on him. His interpretation: he was preoccupied with his psychotherapy and his therapist — whose name was *Bo*nime.

But if the meaning of symbols or of the dream isn't apparent, don't fret about it, says Dr. Krippner. "It's more important that you enjoy your dream than that you correctly analyze it; more important that you learn to appreciate your inner life than that you become an amateur psychoanalyst."

Drs. Krippner, Faraday, and Gershman all stress that the new direction in dream theory and analysis is away from the restricted, sexually defined world of the Freudian dream. They feel that dream symbols express and extend our waking thoughts rather than disguise them to protect us. Training yourself to remember and use your dreams can be a pleasant and helpful day-by-day exercise and should not be distorted into an agonizing probing for sin and guilt.

Only by becoming at ease with your dreams, says Dr. Krippner, can you use them to the fullest, discarding those that seem irrelevant and exploring those that fascinate you and seem related to your life. In some instances the pure pleasure of discovering that we can remember our dreams makes the effort worthwhile. In others, exposing problems that we may have refused to accept consciously can lead to positive, corrective action: or the recognition of emotions that we have tried to submerge can motivate us to accept, or perhaps control or channel them.

THE EXERCISE

Establish a looseleaf notebook right away to begin recording your dreams. This first night, while you are thinking about it, go to bed expecting to remember at least one dream. Immediately upon awakening,

A Fragment of Life

A dream is a fragment of life, broken off at both ends, not connected, either with the part that goes before, or with that which follows after . . . It is a kind of parenthesis inserted in life.

John Wesley

Part of My Own Being

Obviously one must hold oneself responsible for the evil impulses of one's dreams. In what other way can one deal with them? Unless the content of the dream rightly understood is inspired by alien spirits, it is part of my own being.

Sigmund Freud

Dreams are Nature Expressing Something

I was never able to agree with Freud that the dream is a "facade" behind which its meaning lies hidden — a meaning already known but maliciously, so to speak, withheld from consciousness. To me dreams are a part of nature, which harbors no intention to deceive but expresses something as best it can, just as a plant grows or an animal seeks its food as best it can.

C. G. Jung

197

whether in the middle of the night or in the morning, try to capture the dream you were having. Write down a summary that includes both its content and mood. Think about what your emotions were during the dream, and what your feelings about it are now that you are awake.

Don't worry about any deep probing of symbolism for this first dream, but simply enjoy having caught it. If you wish to reflect on its content, go ahead. (It's almost impossible *not* to, once the idea is planted in your head.) But the purpose of this first exercise is simply the experience of touching knowingly, with awareness, that other side of you which you have probably paid little attention to till now.

With this first recorded dream, you have opened the window through which you can now see part of the inner you that has been hidden from view.

24. PROBING INNER CONFLICTS

PREPARATION

Once you have recorded several dreams for the pure purpose of self-awareness, you are ready to put them to work for you as a means to probing some of your inner conflicts. "The dream can reflect and crystallize the dreamer's inner conflicts in relation to the world about him and to himself in a most concise manner," says Dr. Harry Gershman. "The dream can often reveal more than the dreamer is aware of consciously."

It is as though the dream assimilates a kaleidoscope of feelings and reactions from waking life and condenses them, bringing them into focus so that the person reflecting on his dreams can often identify conflicts he did not even realize existed. Many times the dream itself, almost without any symbolism, poses the problem and even points the dreamer toward a solution.

Communications to Ourselves

Both dreams and myths are important communications from ourselves to ourselves. If we do not understand the language in which they are written, we miss a great deal of what we know and tell ourselves in those hours when we are not busy manipulating the outside world.

Erich Fromm

Listen

If you are
in conflict
within your self
have the
different parts
talk out loud
to one another.

Listen
to what they
have to say
to each other.

Feel find out
what they/you
really want
to do.

Bernard Gunther

198

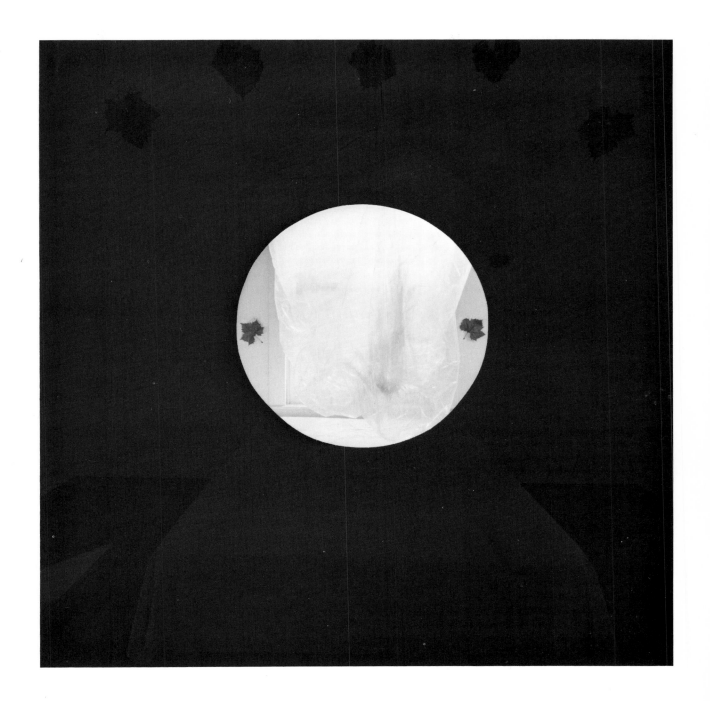

Insane Nightly

The dream is the normal psychosis and dreaming permits each and every one of us to be quietly and safely insane every night of our lives.

Dr. Charles Fischer

The Unsorted Stuff

Sleep is when all the unsorted stuff comes flying out as from a dustbin upset in a high wind.

William Golding
Pincher Martin

Probing Inner Conflict

A skillful man reads his dreams for his self-knowledge . . . However monstrous and grotesque their apparitions, they have a substantial truth.

Ralph Waldo Emerson

When a dream involves symbols, they can reflect any part of the dreamer's life — past, present, future; sexual, social, physical, esthetic, religious. And since the dream and its symbols can communicate on many levels, we should be willing to listen at all levels, without preconceived ideas. Let your mind be completely open — or else you will see only what you are looking for. The greatest value of the dream, Dr. Gershman maintains, is in more accurately depicting what is going on inside a person. Thus, it can assist the dreamer to see the situation, understand it, and meet it more effectively.

However, Dr. Gershman cautions patients not to become so preoccupied with their dreams that they wait for some "secret message" to tell them what to do in crucial situations. Decisions must still be made consciously.

THE EXERCISE

As you now record your dreams, look into them more deeply for insight into any conflicts that you may be having. As you study your dream notes and the emotions surrounding the dreams, think in terms of what conflicts in your life they might be reflecting. Is there some conflict disrupting your life, openly or perhaps half-hidden?

If you reach some conflict-related insight, write down in your notebook what you think it might be. If there are two or more sides to the conflict, write them all down.

Sometimes an insight will be sudden and dramatic . . . "I didn't know I hated him so much!" At other times it will simply reflect two — or three — or four — new sides to a problem, and hold them up to view.

25. SEXUAL DREAMS

PREPARATION

Don't ever feel guilty about your sex dreams. Everyone has them to one degree or another, though some are more exciting or intricate than others. View them calmly and with perspective.

Some people dream to orgasm; others do not. Some wake up from a sexual dream and are so excited by it that they masturbate to orgasm while awake.

Sex dreams may be triggered by some stimulus from a book or movie seen during the day, or by something as physical as a full bladder or tight clothing, or simply by a build-up of sexual tension not recently released.

Here are a number of ways to understand sexual dreams.

THE EXERCISE

1. Sex dreams can be fun and you can look at them for pure entertainment value.

2. Or you can use them to try to achieve added insights concerning your sexual feelings that could lead to a more satisfying sex life.

If, for example, a certain sexual situation keeps recurring in your dreams, it could be evidence that this situation is one of particular concern and conflict, or it could mean that here is an area that you are more interested in than you realized.

If you think a sexual dream reflects concern and conflict, this may be due to an inability to master the situation enacted, or one symbolically like it. Think about the situation, and try to determine whether any past experiences, or parental attitudes, or other factors in your background may be influencing your attitude and response.

Sex Dreams and Education

Kinsey found a high relationship between educational level and frequency of nocturnal emissions. More than 99 per cent of college students have emission dreams at some time, 85 per cent of those with a high school education do, and 75 per cent of those with grade school education. In fact, during adolescence the boys who eventually went to college had seven times more wet dreams than the boys who did not continue past grade school!

A sleep fact

Children and Sexual Dreams

It seems to be my fate to discover only the obvious; that children have sexual feelings, which every nursemaid knows; and that night dreams are just as much wish-fulfillment as daydreams.

Sigmund Freud

If you think that a dream situation keeps recurring because it represents something you secretly desire, you may consider carrying it out in your waking life — assuming that it is not harmful in any way. But if you believe deep down that you probably enjoy fantasizing about it more than you would enjoy doing it, then go ahead and allow the fantasy to enact itself.

3. Sometimes your sex dreams reflect how you, at a deep level, actually feel about sex. When you wake up from a sex dream, think about the emotions you felt while you were having the dream, then consider your emotions while reviewing the dream awake, and compare them. If you had any feelings of fear, resentment, or frustration, these may provide a key to some underlying attitudes about sex that you might wish to change.

Something to Consider

A dream which is not interpreted is like a letter which is not read.

THE TALMUD

26. PROBLEM SOLVING

PREPARATION

Many a person has gone to sleep with a problem on his mind and awakened in the morning with the solution. Somehow, through the night, our unconscious mind seems to filter the facts differently, looking at the problem in a new way or with keener insight than our conscious brain was able to do.

In an attempt to analyze this phenomenon, Dr. Dement once gave a brain-twister type problem to a group of volunteers in his sleep laboratory and found that a significant number of them dreamed about the correct answer, although some of them did not recognize it for what it was. So, in order to use dreams for problem solving, we must be alert to what they are telling us. Sometimes the answer comes through in a straightforward way, sometimes symbolically.

And always there is the danger of our waking up with a superb answer which we don't write down immediately and have forgotten by the time we get around to it.

An Encouraging Omen

Then he told of a curious dream which he had at Biarritz. He had, he said, been ascending a mountain path, which grew even narrower till at last he came to a high wall, at its side being a deep abyss. For a moment he stood reflecting whether he should not turn back; but then he struck out with his walking-stick at the wall, which at once disappeared, leaving his path open and unimpeded—an encouraging omen, he added, for the difficulties that were in store for him.

OTTO, PRINCE VON BISMARCK

Graham Wallas, in *The Art of Thought,* describes four stages of creative thinking and problem solving: *preparation,* in which the person works intensely on the problem; *incubation,* in which the problem is temporarily put aside while the person does something else; *illumination* or insight, when the person suddenly sees how the problem can be solved; and *verification* or revision, in which he works out the details of the solution.

These four stages can apply equally well to problems solved in sleep: you work on the problem during your waking hours, and sleep becomes the incubation period. Illumination occurs upon waking up.

Perhaps we had the solutions in our waking mind all the time, but missed it because of all the noise; our dreams may simply eliminate distractions and allow us to see the solution.

In any event, this method does seem to work often, if not always. When it doesn't work, it can be frustrating and tormenting if the problem is serious. Sometimes it can be funny.

Dorothy Parker once dreamed she had found *the* answer to the problem of the universe. She woke up, wrote it down, and in the morning found "Hoggamous, higgamous, men are polygamous. Higgamous, hoggamous, women monogamous."

THE EXERCISE

When you have a problem to solve or a decision to make, consider various facets of the problem off and on during the day, trying to put into your brain every fact and feeling, every advantage and disadvantage, all the alternate possibilities involved. Don't just glide over the problem; think about it consciously in depth.

When you get into bed, go over the facts once more, as if you were feeding information into a computer. Then, as you fall asleep, tell your brain to work on the problem in your dreams. Keep your mind as open as

Integrate Your Dream

The Gestalt approach is to integrate dreams rather than to analyze them. Integrating can be accomplished by consciously reliving the dream, by taking responsibility for being the objects and people in the dream, by becoming aware of the messages the dream holds. To learn from dreams, it is not essential to work out an entire dream. Working with small bits of the dream is often fruitful.

Muriel James and Dorothy Jongeward

possible, to allow innovative thoughts to enter. When you awaken in the morning, lie still and immediately try to capture your dream and waking thoughts to see if you have reached some insight.

NOTE

In sum, don't depend on your dreams to give you automatic answers to important problems, but help them by keeping an open mind, a mind receptive to new thoughts.

Free from the Human Prison

Dreams are excursions into the limbo of things, a semi-deliverance from the human prison.

Henri Amiel

205

27. THE CREATIVE DREAM

PREPARATION

Robert Louis Stevenson wrote many of his works as a result of dreams. In fact, he trained himself to dream plots for his stories. The plot of *Dr. Jekyll and Mr. Hyde* was one of his many dream-inspired creations.

Samuel Taylor Coleridge wrote large portions of *Kubla Khan* in his sleep. Thackeray couldn't think of a title for his new novel about a girl named Becky Sharp. The title finally came to him in a dream. "I jumped out of bed in the middle of the night, ran three times around my room, uttering Vanity Fair, Vanity Fair, Vanity Fair."

The Swedish playwright, Strindberg, said, "I believe in dreams, for my brain works sharpest when I am asleep."

Voltaire dreamed a whole canto of *La Henriade.*

Guiseppe Tartini wrote down his famous "Devil's Sonata" after he heard it played by the devil on a violin in a dream. Richard Wagner said of his opera *Tristan and Isolde,* that, "I dreamed all this: never could my poor head have invented such a thing purposely."

Dreams have also played a large part in the field of scientific discovery and invention. Elias Howe, the inventor of the sewing machine, worked for years on his invention, but could not figure out where to put the eyes in the sewing machine needles to make them work. One night he dreamed that he was captured by a tribe of savages who commanded him on "pain of death" to finish the machine. As the savages surrounded him and raised their spears for the kill, he saw that the heads of the spears had eye-shaped

Dr. Jekyll and Mr. Hyde

I had long been trying to write a story on this subject, the *Strange Case of Dr. Jekyll and Mr. Hyde,* to find a body, a vehicle, for that strong sense of man's double being which must at times come in upon and overwhelm the mind of every thinking creature . . . For two days I went about racking my brains for a plot of any sort; and on the second night I dreamed the scene at the window, and a scene afterward split in two, in which Hyde, pursued for some crime, took the powder and underwent the change in the presence of his pursuers. All the rest was made awake and consciously . . .

Robert Louis Stevenson

206

holes. He had solved the problem: what he needed was a needle with an eye near the point! He woke up, got out of bed, and made the needle he needed.

Dr. Niels Bohr, the renowned physicist, evolved his theory of electrons revolving around atoms after he dreamed of a sun with planets attached by strings revolving around it.

Dr. F. A. Kekule von Stadonitz dreamed of atoms twisting and turning like snakes. Suddenly one snake seized its own tail and whirled about; this gave him the concept of the structure of a benzene ring — one of the basic structures of organic substances found throughout the world.

Albert Einstein's concept for his theory of relativity is said to have come to him while he was dozing in bed, sick.

While working on lead shot for guns, inventor James Watt had a recurring dream of walking through a heavy storm — not of water, but of lead pellets. He interpreted this as meaning that molten lead falling through air would harden into round pellets. To test this hypothesis, he went up into a church tower and threw melted lead into the water far below. The lead did form round pellets on hitting the water — which completely changed the lead shot industry.

Dreams are potentially creative experiences but not just for artists, scientists and inventors; all of us can use them creatively.

Deep in the Malay Peninsula lives the Senoi tribe, isolated, surrounded by jungle. They are remarkably free of mental illness, community conflict, and violent

Inventive Dreaming

On the 2nd of June, 1789, being tired with walking, he sat down on a chair, about nine in the evening, to enjoy a short slumber; but scarcely had he closed his eyes, when the image of an instrument such as he wished for, seemed to present itself before him, and terrified him so much that he awoke as if he had been struck with an electric shock. He immediately started up in a kind of enthusiasm; and made a series of experiments which convinced him that what he had seen was perfectly right,— that he now had it in his power to carry it into execution. He made his experiments, and constructed his first instrument in so private a manner, that no person knew anything of it. On the 8th of March, 1790, his first instrument of this kind was completed, and in a few days he was able to play on it some easy pieces of music. To this instrument he gave the name of _Euphon_, which signifies an instrument which has a pleasant sound.

Dr. Ernst Chladni
1756–1827

crime. Dr. Kilton Stewart, who has studied them extensively, believes this is largely due to the tribe's creative use of dreams: the Senois train themselves from infancy to act out positive dreams and neutralize negative ones.

"Breakfast in the Senoi house," says Dr. Stewart, "is like a dream clinic." If a Senoi man dreams that a friend is an enemy, he will tell his friend about it so he can repair the negative dream image by friendly exchange, rather than repressing his negative thoughts.

We can use our dreams regularly in the same way — to show us new ways of doing things and new ways to affect our relationships with others and to act out the daily events of our lives.

THE EXERCISE

While falling asleep, open your mind to whatever creative thoughts flow through it. On awakening, always record your dreams in the notebook you started, and each day examine your dreams for creative ideas that could be put to use.

If you dream something about a friend or a relative, use it as a conversational gambit. Talk over the dream with the person concerned and discuss your relationship in terms of the dream. Your dreams can thus be used to get to know your fellowman better and to help establish close and meaningful communication.

Suggestibility

Normal suggestibility and normal auto-suggestibility are an integral part of our mental mechanism and play a decisive role in whatever we think, feel and do.

Margaret Steger

28. CATCHING DAYDREAMS

PREPARATION

At one point during astronaut Walter Schirra's Mercury space flight, the ground control station tried three times unsuccessfully to contact him in the orbiting space capsule. When contact was finally made, ground control asked what was wrong. "I guess," said Schirra, "I was daydreaming."

Although most of us daydream, we tend to be a little embarrassed by the habit and almost never take advantage of it. In fact, we often actively try to break our children of it. Actually, daydreams can be very useful. As scientists study them, they are learning that daydreaming is of greater significance to human development than anyone had suspected.

Freud was one of the first to observe their importance, and in 1907 pointed out that the imaginative play of children is preserved in the form of daydreaming in adults. Most adults conceal their fantasies, Freud said, but indulge in them when experiencing some

Known in a Vision

Hear my words: If there is a prophet among you, I the Lord make myself known to him in a vision, I speak with him in a dream. Not so with my servant Moses; he is entrusted with all my house. With him I speak mouth to mouth, clearly, and not in dark speech; and he beholds the form of the Lord.

Numbers 12:6-8

dissatisfaction or unhappiness. Later, Anna Freud, his daughter, extended his theory and listed daydreaming as one of the significant ways of avoiding anxiety and dealing with conflicts.

Today, researchers are trying to zero in on this habit, and even use a General Daydream Questionnaire to learn what people's daydreams are about, and how often and under what circumstances they occur. They have found that daydreaming is indulged in by practically everyone — child or adult. Daydreams reach a peak in frequency around adolescence and early adulthood, then taper off somewhat. In one survey of college-educated adults, most reported that they had fairly sharp and vivid daydreams, that these took place most often when they were alone or just before going to sleep, and that many dealt with practical matters like "how to increase my income next year." A high percentage said their daydreams centered on sexual satisfaction, imaginary good fortune, and such altruistic concerns as "peace for the world." In older persons, they usually center around relived memories.

Scientists stress that daydreaming is healthy. In fact, children who *don't* daydream or who rarely indulge in imaginative play seem more likely to be hyperactive, disruptive and inattentive, and to have little direction or purpose. Children who use a great deal of fantasy and daydream frequently were found to be clearly superior in creativity and motivation for achievement. Low-fantasy children had less insight, were less subtle, less close to their parents and more interested in physical activity than in mental work.

Experimenters believe that daydreaming is only one manifestation of a use of fantasy that is basic to human growth.

Preludes of the Truth

Maybe the wildest dreams are but the needful preludes of the truth.

Alfred Lord Tennyson

THE EXERCISE

The first step is to realize that you are a daydreamer, and have always been. Take a few moments to recapture some of your favorite ones.

When you were younger, did you often rehearse an event in fantasy before it happened? Did you imagine how you would act in public, or visualize yourself as an adult, or dream of future good times?

As a teenager, did you use daydreaming to work out career choices, education, marriage? Did you envision yourself as an athletic hero, a corporation president, or part of a great romance? You probably acted out a dozen plots with a dozen endings to each. Relive some of them now to see how important they were to you then.

The second step is to realize that you can still use daydreams to good effect by rehearsing upcoming social or business situations, things pleasant or things unpleasant.

Practice using your daydreams constructively during moments of boredom, or quiet, at tedious meetings, or while waiting for an appointment.

NOTE

Help children be creative by encouraging imaginative play and daydreams. Help young people by respecting their need to be alone to wonder and to daydream.

Our Whole Life and Fate

These whimsical pictures, inasmuch as they originate from us, may well have an analogy with our whole life and fate.

Goethe

213

29. DREAMS AND ESP

PREPARATION

Some people are more receptive to ESP experiences than others. Usually a person strong in extrasensory perception is also easily hypnotized, tuned in to other people, relaxed, and receptive.

ESP includes three basic experiences: (1) *clairvoyance and clairaudience* (the ability to see or hear things that are out of sight and out of normal hearing range), (2) *telepathy* (reading another person's thoughts), and (3) *precognition* (foretelling a future event).

All of these experiences have been shown to be possible, indeed fairly common, in dreams. Dr. Louisa Rhine, of the Institute for Parapsychology in Durham, North Carolina, has collected more than 10,000 case histories suggesting ESP in different types of people. Sixty-five per cent of the experiences were reported as having taken place in dreams.

In fact, so much validity is being found in dream predictions that a Central Premonitions Registry has been set up in New York City to serve as a clearing-house for people who have what they think are pre-cognitive dreams and wish to place them on record. (They should be sent there *before* the predicted event takes place.)

Psychologist Rhea White, of the American Society for Psychical Research in New York, says that the conditions that appear to be essential to successful ESP are: deep mental and physical relaxation, lack of strain, passiveness, and the ability to "blank out" the mind.

If you find, as you keep track of your dreams, that you have premonitions of events to come or seem to pick up other people's thoughts, do not become alarmed; accept these experiences as an enhancement of your life, and use the dreams in whatever positive ways that suggest themselves. If you receive a very strong inner warning not to do something, then perhaps you should not do it. If you feel that someone very much wants to speak to you or is thinking about you, pick up the phone and find out if you were on

Fulfilled Dreams

Dreams which have come to pass are always predictions which no one can doubt, no account being taken of dreams which are never fulfilled.

Voltaire

Relating to Future Events

A number of observations strongly suggest the presence of truly precognitive elements in the manifest dream content. It seems to contain "bits" of information relating to future events, not based on rational inference and not amenable to interpretation in terms of telepathic self-fulfillment.

Dr. Jan Ehrenwald

that person's mind, and why. If there are strong emotional ties between you, you will find in a surprising number of instances that your inner prompting was correct.

Dr. Stanley Krippner believes that we'll eventually have to revise our image of man on the basis of telepathic evidence. He feels the present psychological view of man as alienated and cut off from his surroundings may soon disappear.

"Telepathy may teach us that in the basic fabric of life everything and everyone is linked, that man is continuously enmeshed, that he is always an integral part of all life on the face of the earth."

THE EXERCISE

Test yourself for extrasensory perception. Have a friend pick out a painting or photograph from a magazine — one that has strong colors or strong emotional impact. He is not to tell you *anything* about it, not even where he got it. Arrange for a specific time that you will go to sleep. About two hours after that time, he should begin to concentrate deeply on the picture, trying to send it to your mind. If the picture is something like a waterfall, he might turn on the shower; if it is a flag, he could get a toy flag and wave it. He should use anything — no matter how silly — that will strengthen the signals coming to you. At any time you wake up at night, and when you wake up in the morning, record your dream impressions down to the tiniest detail. Check with your friend to see if there are any correlations.

A variation of this experiment is to have someone put a picture in an envelope without telling you what it is. He seals the envelope tightly. You put it under your pillow when you go to bed, and as you go to sleep try to concentrate on what is in the envelope, pulling out its feelings and images. When you wake up both at night and in the morning, write down your dream notes. Then, with your morning coffee, after you have read over your notes again, open the envelope and look at the picture. Go through your notes and see if you picked up anything in the way of shapes, colors, moods, or actual persons or objects in the scene.

The Shadows of Real Events

Dreams full oft are found of real events the forms and shadows.

Joanna Baillie

Clearly in Dreams

Why does the eye see a thing more clearly in dreams than the imagination when awake?

Leonardo da Vinci

216

30. DREAM CONTROL

PREPARATION

Almost everyone can learn the principles of progressive relaxation and thus assume control of the process of falling asleep. A surprising number of people can also control their dreams.

Some of these people seem to be aware that they are dreaming even while they are dreaming, and can talk to themselves in relation to that knowledge, even to the point of controlling the direction and plot of the dream.

Dreams and the Mind

If we can understand dreams, we'll be that much closer to understanding the human mind in general.

Dr. Joseph Muzio

One woman, on waking up frightened from a bad dream, tells herself she is a dingbat, purposefully turns over to the other side, and directs her mind to the most beautiful, peaceful painting she can imagine. Whenever something unpleasant begins to intrude upon the scene, she forces it away until her mind finally is at peace again.

A ten-year-old boy handles his bad dreams in an even more forceful manner. He bangs his head — we hope gently — against the wall; this, he says, turns off the dream completely.

An eight-year-old girl who suffered from frequent dreams about scary monsters was instructed to approach them in her dreams and make friends with them.

Many people who can change the directions of their dreams can also wake themselves up from a dream at will. They do so if the dream is unpleasant, or if they have some creative insight during the dream, or a solution to a problem.

THE EXERCISE

Even if you do not have complete control over your dreams, you can still counteract the images of bad dreams after you wake up.

Either immediately or later in the day when you have a free moment, close your eyes and think of the dream, vividly picturing the most frightening thing about it. Look at it carefully. Now, still with your eyes closed, make an attempt to befriend the thing. Think up a gift it might like, and present it to him. Take the thing by the hand and point out various interesting sights to it. Invite it to sit down and share an ice cream soda.

After a while you will find that frightening dreams become less and less frequent.

To Switch Dreams

When I want to switch dreams, I simply blink my eyes and change the channel.

Bob Linde
Age 10

If There Were Dreams to Sell

If there were dreams to sell,
What would you buy?
Some cost a passing bell;
Some a light sigh,
That shakes from Life's fresh crown
Only a rose-leaf down.
If there were dreams to sell,
Merry and sad to tell,
And the crier rang the bell,
What would you buy?

Thomas Lovell Beddoes

31. CHILDREN'S DREAMS

PREPARATION

When children of the Senoi tribe have a dream of falling, their parents try to turn the fearful dream into a positive one. When the child tells about it at the dream conversations in the morning, the parent will say something like, "That is a wonderful dream. Where did you fall to and what did you discover there?" The fear of falling can thus be turned into the joy of flying, or at least into a neutral appreciation of the event.

THE EXERCISE

Listen to what your child tells you about his dreams. What he says can often be a clue to things that are bothering him, and you can use the occurrence of the dream as a means for talking a problem through.

If your child wakes up in the middle of the night screaming that monsters or people are chasing him, don't just tell him not to be silly, that there are no monsters. But talk about it. If he says there is somebody under the bed, say "Let's look together and see if there is anything there." If he says he saw a face, ask him if he could tell whose face it was. If he says he saw a monster, ask him what the monster was doing. If it was chasing him, ask him if he has any idea why the monster was chasing him. Perhaps he feels guilty about something.

Encourage your children to report their dreams at the breakfast table. When they do, don't jump to quick conclusions, but explore the dream together. Ask them why they think they had that particular dream. Suggest that they expand on the idea, or even act out what one of the characters was like. It can turn a formerly scary part of their life into something that is tension-releasing and interesting.

Off to Dreamland

Wynken, Blynken, and Nod one night
    Sailed off in a wooden shoe —
Sailed on a river of crystal light
    Into a sea of dew.

        Eugene Field
        Wynken, Blynken, and Nod

Children's Dreams

In their symbolic structure as well as in their content, children's dreams seem to be closely related to symbolic play. It is unnecessary to stress the differences — they are obvious. The dreamer believes what he dreams, while belief in the pretence of play is always very relative. The construction of games is much more deliberately controlled, while that of dreams carries the subject far beyond the point his conscious would wish. Most important of all, in play, material substitutes of all kinds which make it easier to imagine the object are used as symbols, while in dreams the object must be represented by a mental image or by another image symbolising the same object.

        Jean Piaget

And as you tell them of your dreams, they will also learn that dreams are not something that happens just to them, but that they are a universal experience.

Talking about dreams will show your child that they can be dealt with and that they are an acceptable part of each person's life. And by exploring dreams, he will learn to be in touch with his inner self.

And I Ate Myself

One time I dreamt I was a hamburger. And I ate myself up.

**Michael Black
Age 9**

About the Photographer

Murray Riss was born in Poland in 1940. Currently Assistant Professor of Art at the Memphis Academy of Art, he studied at City College of the City University of New York, B.A., 1963, and Rhode Island School of Design, M.F.A., 1968.

His exhibitions include "Recent Acquisitions", Museum of Modern Art, New York, 1970; "Vision and Expression", George Eastman House, Rochester, New York, 1969; Chicago Art Institute, 1971; University of Iowa, 1971; Minneapolis Institute of Fine Arts, 1971; "Portraits", Moore College of Art, Philadelphia, 1972; "Contemporary Photographers VII", George Eastman House, 1973; one-man exhibition sponsored by Visual Studies Workshop, State University of New York at Buffalo (Rochester), New York, 1974.

Publications by Murray Riss include "Vision and Expression", Horizon Press, 1969; "Photography as Art", Vol. 10, Time-Life Library of Photography; "First Wave", Modern Photography, June 1972.

Page 17

Page 20

Page 29

Page 52

Page 61

Page 70

Page 79

Page 80

Page 84

Page 111

Page 124

Page 146

Page 183

Certain photographic illustrations appearing in this book are details taken from complete photographs. The images in their entirety are reproduced here with the accompanying page numbers on which the details appear.

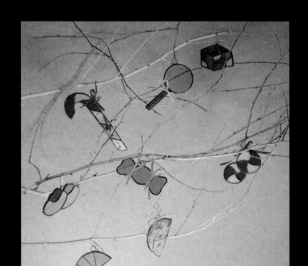

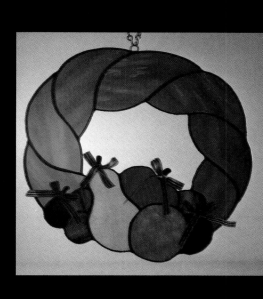

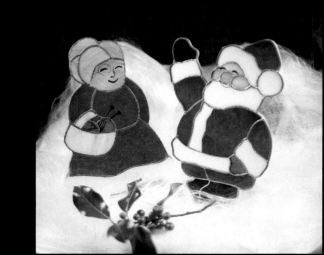

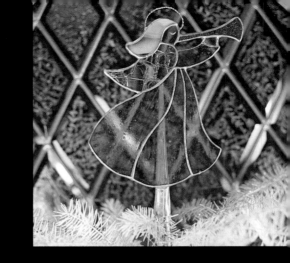